Christine Liao was born and educated in Melbourne. A graduate of Melbourne University she has done extensive research into modern Chinese literature, much of it in China, which she has visited on three occasions.

She lectured at Melbourne University from 1969 to 1980 and then joined the Australia-China Council as an interpreter. During her year with the Council she met many leading Chinese publishers and academics and became increasingly aware of the lack of English translations of recent Chinese writing.

At present Christine Liao is a lecturer in Chinese literature at the Canberra College of Advanced Education and she is the Executive Secretary of the Australian Association of Chinese Artists which promotes the work of Chinese artists living in Australia and of Australian artists who paint in traditional Chinese style.

She lives with her husband and son in Melbourne.

THE FONTANA
COLLECTION OF
MODERN CHINESE WRITING

Edited by Christine M. Liao

FONTANA/COLLINS

in association with The Chinese Literature Publishing House of
Beijing

First published in Fontana Books, 1983
Printed and bound in Australia by
The Dominion Press–Hedges & Bell, Melbourne

National Library of Australia
Cataloguing-in-Publication

   The Fontana collection of modern Chinese writing.

   ISBN 0 00 636558 2

   1. Chinese literature – 20th century –
   Translations into English.   2. English literature –
   Translations from Chinese.   I. Liao, Christine M.

895.1'08'005

ACKNOWLEDGEMENTS

Stories for inclusion in this collection have been selected by Yang Xianyi, Gladys Yang and members of the staff of *Chinese Literature*. Responsibility for the Introduction, for selection and translation of the poetry, all but the poems of Shu Ting, and of the notes on the authors, rests with the editor.

We express particular gratitude to Professor Huang Yongyu for the cover.

CONTENTS

Introduction

A society comes to life through its literature. In the last five years China has been experiencing an unprecedented surge in literary publishing. There are estimates of some six hundred journals and magazines that publish literature exclusively or incorporate stories, novels, poems and literary criticism. Many of these began publication in 1978 and 1979 but many are revivals of journals which were forced to cease publication with the onset the Cultural Revolution (1966–76).

Some journals, such as *People's Literature*, *Poetry* and *The Literary Gazette*, are representative of national literary circles. Others are linked to a province or region, still others are associated with Chinese departments at the universities. In some cases, an author whose work is controversial may have a contentious work rejected by one of the regular publishing outlets but will find it acceptable to a provincial journal, especially if the writer is well known.

This richness has been largely unavailable to the English-speaking world, since very little of it has been translated into English and still less, published overseas. Yet it is precisely these last few years that are the most interesting, since they constitute a period of experiment with 'new' literary forms and subjects as well as a reaction to the excessive stringencies and repression of earlier periods, in particular the Cultural Revolution and the earlier 'anti-Rightist' campaign (1957). As well as the usual subjects of life in the countryside and the factories, Chinese poets and writers are once more writing of love between the sexes, of the competing roles of parents and the workplace in courtship and marriage and the burden of the middle-aged. They are taking a critical look at their society and seeking to discover what went wrong to allow the 'ten year holocaust', as it is sometimes described, to occur.

Some writers are experimenting with forms and concepts derived from modern American and European literature. Even science fiction is becoming a popular genre. In some cases such experiments are regarded with caution. Many trends, such as explicit treatment of sex, are seen as undesirable and there is a campaign underway against pornography in all the arts, but pornography defined much more rigorously than the word is applied in the West. They are also turning back to the twenties and thirties to seek inspiration from the early writers who led Chinese literature out of the classical past.

It is characteristic of writing in China that most writers are members of the Writers' Association. Many, especially ethnic and professional writers, have been actively assisted in their careers by the Association. They have often received training in their craft by organs of the association and are sometimes given particular writing assignments to carry out. There are many exceptions, but broadly speaking, it is possible to construct a rough profile of a modern Chinese writer which would fit many of them. He (for 'he' read 'he or she') might be in his forties or early fifties. Writing may be a spare time activity but is more usually a regular occupation for which he draws a salary. As a member, sometimes an official, in a regional or central writers' association, he may also be an administrator. He is probably of poor peasant background and had an early fondness for and exposure to popular literary or entertainment forms; perhaps a parent or grandparent who sang or was a story-teller (Malqinhu) or 'cross-talk' entertainer (Li Huiwen's grandfather was a 'shadow-show' puppeteer). He mostly had little formal education, primary school and possibly some secondary schooling.

He may have participated early in Communist-led activities such as the Youth League, and from there entered the cultural wing of the organization where he may have trained as a reporter and field worker.

After 1949 and during the fifties, he probably engaged in

cultural activities and reporting. His work was usually oriented to support the current campaigns—among them in the fifties land reform and collectivization. Frequently, he achieved a position in the Writers' Association often at provincial level. In many cases, he suffered during the 'anti-Rightist' campaign, despite an 'impeccable' class background.

In the sixties, especially during the Cultural Revolution, he was probably removed from office and sent to work in rural areas where he was unable to write. Rehabilitation for such people usually began in 1977.

The stories themselves may be read for their intrinsic interest as stories well told, however literature in this realist mode is also social commentary and can be read for what it tells us of the society and its people reassessing values after a period of great social and political turmoil and individual suffering.

This role of social comment, in some cases exposé, is a feature shared by all the stories in the anthology. This is not to say that they are in any way dissenting or underground literature. They need to be seen in the context of the current political attitude to literature that is being promoted by Chinese literary authorities. Some comments made by the famous old novelist Bajin, now chairman of the Writers' Association, on the occasion of the 1979 literary awards, are instructive here. He notes:

> Writers can write about what they know but they should also keep on learning what is new in life. Now the crux of the Party's work has shifted to socialist modernization. Our lives are changing, our people are progressing. If we do not integrate ourselves with the new period and the new people, if we do not learn and are not familiar with the new life, our works will fail to satisfy the needs of the times . . . It has been proved that the method of forcing them all to the grassroots level without any distinction did not work. Authors should be allowed to choose their own 'base in life'.
>
> Apart from learning from life, from people, we need also to stress learning from books. It is very important to learn scientific and cultural knowledge, to learn from superior literary works, both old and new, Chinese and foreign, so as

> to raise our cultural level and artistic taste.
>   Indeed we see the influence of such superior literary works
> from China and overseas in some of these stories.

A great deal about recent changes in the Chinese literary world
is implicit in these remarks and in the rest of Bajin's statement.
They allude to the restrictive policies of the Cultural
Revolution that required all writers to experience a stint in the
countryside, actually living the peasants' way of life. They
imply the present relaxation set in train on 4 February 1979
with the release of Zhou Enlai's speech. This had been
delivered much earlier on 19 June 1961.

In it he had called for the relaxation of control over writing.
It was followed by a rash of responses from writers calling for
greater freedom, and was the first step in the current revival of
the so-called 'Hundred Flowers', an echo of the earlier policy of
1956. Under this policy, writers are encouraged to express
their ideas about any subject they will. However, they must be
prepared to have their work assessed and criticized, if the
subjects they do write about are very controversial.

Another feature of the literary scene is the award system.
The system applies not only to stories, but also to drama and
film. Awards are given in two categories—first and second—
for the most superior examples of a short-story, novella (the
Chinese word is *zhongpian xiaoshuo*, medium-length novel and
approximates to the German novella in length), novel, play and
film. The subjects are voted for by the readers of the relevant
literary or art publications, although the popular choice is
finally vetted by a panel of judges from the respective
association. *People's Literature, Popular Cinema,* and other
organs of the Writers' or Film Associations print entry forms in
their journals.

This anthology is a representative one in more than one
sense. Issues that are explored through the characters in these
stories are not restricted to life in the cities or to rural China,
neither do they describe only the workers and peasants.
Intellectual concerns are aired as well. Not only are the authors
some of China's most interesting and promising writers, they
come from diverse ethnic backgrounds. The famous Mongolian

writer, Malqinhu, who is best known for his 'Tales of the Kolqin Prairies', writes of the Lhama Buddhist rites that can transform a young boy into a god overnight. Other writers, although themselves Han Chinese, have lived and worked among the minority races. Thus the destructive superstition that a ghost may take over the personality of a man or woman, which is a disturbing part of Dai folklore, is the subject chosen by Yang Zhao and Bai Hanghu, who are themselves an unusual phenomenon; a husband and wife writing team who have lived and worked in the province of Yunnan, in far south-west China that has a common border with Vietnam.

Stories by both men and women writers are included. Indeed the most moving and dramatic of these, *At Middle Age,* is written by a woman, Shen Rong. She was virtually unknown as a writer until this was published in the journal *Harvest*. It won national acclaim and was voted the best story of the 1977–79 period, when the literary award system was introduced in 1979. The story touched a chord with Chinese readers, especially middle-aged intellectuals, who had had to bear the brunt of the opprobrium and suffering during the ten years of the Cultural Revolution—in many instances longer than that—and who were now being called upon to contribute their skills, so indispensable if the country was to be set back on its feet again.

Politics and literature interact very closely in China. Changes in the official attitude to poets, writers and other intellectuals have become a reliable barometer of changes in the political line. Thus during the Cultural Revolution, they were 'stinking category nine', but now after the Twelfth Party Congress they actually join the workers, peasants and soldiers among the proletariat.

Both the stories and poems selected for inclusion in the anthology reflect the society itself, its ideals and the political and social changes that have moulded it during the last twenty years. Sometimes the reflection is a mirror image, sometimes, as in the 'Colosseum of Ancient Rome', the poem is about the barbarity of another culture and another age and yet there is clearly a dimension to it which carries a forceful suggestion of events nearer to hand. Thus 'the nobles . . . their eating utensils . . . stained with blood', and the lines that describe the 'brains' behind the 'roughnecks' or hired hands of the Colosseum:

> *These roughnecks receive their instructions from others*
> *Who don't kill directly,*
> *Yet are more sinister than executioners*

point to events and personages of the 1966–76 period; the Gang of Four.

The diversity of the writing that has appeared in the last four or five years, its relatively outspoken and critical appraisal of the society, make this a highly significant time for Chinese literature. The buoyant state of publishing and the enthusiasm with which young poets and writers are working, augurs well for the years to come.

Poetry in the Anthology

Poetry in the modern idiom has kept pace with the expansion in writing generally. Much new poetry is experimental. Themes that in the period of repression were denied to writers are once again acceptable and large quantities of diverse and interesting verse are appearing all the time. Rather than attempt to survey this large corpus, the quality of which varies considerably from poet to poet, this anthology includes only a very few works of other poets and concentrates on some recent work of one man; the well-established poet Ai Qing. He is considered by many critics to be China's foremost living poet. The small selection of other verse includes two poems by the poetess Shu Ting and three satires by the artist and occasional poet, Huang Yongyu.

Stories

Shen Rong

Shen Rong, born in the thriving river port of Hankou in Hubei province but brought up in Sichuan, regards herself as Sichuanese. Like many other modern authors, initially she had little formal education. She began working with only one year of secondary schooling behind her, but was associated early on with books, as her first job was that of shop assistant in a bookshop in Chongqing, capital of Sichuan. That was 1951. After a year there, she went to the South-west and worked for the *Workers' Daily News* in the Letters to the Editor section. She must also have been educating herself in her spare time, since she passed the Universities' Entrance Examination in 1954 and began to study Russian. She was later to work as a Russian interpreter and as a secondary school teacher. It is safe to assume that in the course of her training in Russian, she read some important Russian literature, at least in the period before the Sino-Soviet split in 1960. (Students in interpreters' courses are always encouraged to read as widely as possible in the target language.)

Shen Rong, in a brief biography for the Peking Publishing

House, wrote of her early life:

> My childhood was no pastoral idyll. I had no enviable record
> of scholarship, no heroic career of struggle. My days were
> spent in a very ordinary way.

She began writing in 1964, some two years before the Cultural
Revolution began. The publication of this story, *At Middle Age,*
in the bi-monthly journal *Harvest* in January 1980, established
Shen Rong as a writer. The novella won her first prize in the
competition held by the Writers' Association for the best
medium-length work written between 1977 and 1979. This
addresses the issues of injustice and pressure endured by
highly educated, middle-aged Chinese during the years of
political and social upheaval. They had been constrained to
work long hours under very poor working conditions and with
meagre rates of pay, and yet are the very people most in
demand in the current drive for scientific and technical
modernization. Shen Rong acknowledged that she had a
conscious, didactic purpose in writing this story of the woman
oculist, Lu Wenting:

> It was my intention, through the medium of a novella, to
> elicit society's concern for their difficult situation and in this
> way to fulfill a certain responsibility that I have.

The appeal to the readership lies, if anything, more in the
writer's consummate literary skills and her insight into her
characters than in its treatment of these social issues. Shen
Rong has been writing prolifically. She has the full length
novels *Forever Young* and *Light and Darkness* to her credit, as
well as four novellas, including *Truth and Falsehood,* and
various short stories.

Shen Rong
At Middle Age

Were the stars twinkling in the sky? Was a boat rocking on the sea? Lu Wenting, an oculist, lay on her back in hospital. Circles of light, bright or dim, appeared before her eyes. She seemed to be lifted by a cloud, up and down, drifting about without any direction.

Was she dreaming or dying?

She remembered vaguely going to the operating theatre that morning, putting on her operating gown and walking over to the wash-basin. Ah, yes, Jiang Yafen, her good friend, had volunteered to be her assistant. Having got their visas, Jiang and her family were soon leaving for Canada. This was their last operation as colleagues.

Together they washed their hands. They had been medical students in the same college in the fifties and, after graduation, had been assigned to the same hospital. As friends and colleagues for more than twenty years, they found it hard to part. This was no mood for a doctor to be in prior to an operation. Lu remembered she had wanted to say something to ease their sadness. What had she said? She had turned to Jiang and inquired, 'Have you booked your plane tickets, Yafen?'

What had been her reply? She had said nothing, but her eyes had gone red. Then after a long time Jiang asked, 'You think you can manage three operations in one morning?'

Lu couldn't remember what she had answered. She had probably gone on scrubbing her nails in silence. The new brush hurt her fingertips. She looked at the soap bubbles on her hands and glanced at the clock on the wall, strictly following the rules, brushing her hands, wrists and arms three

times, three minutes each. Ten minutes later she soaked her
arms in a pail of antiseptic, 75 per çent alcohol. It was white—
maybe yellowish. Even now her hands and arms were numb
and burning. From the alcohol? No. It was unlikely. They had
never hurt before. Why couldn't she lift them?

She remembered that at the start of the operation, when she
had injected novocaine behind the patient's eyeball, Yafen had
asked softly, 'Has your daughter got over her pneumonia?'

What was wrong with Jiang today? Didn't she know that
when operating a surgeon should forget everything, including
herself and her family, and concentrate on the patient? How
could she inquire after Xiaojia at such a time? Perhaps, feeling
miserable about leaving, she had forgotten that she was
assisting at an operation.

A bit annoyed, Lu retorted, 'I'm only thinking about this eye
now.'

She lowered her head and cut with a pair of curved scissors.

One operation after another. Why three in one morning? She
had had to remove Vice-minister Jiao's cataract, transplant a
cornea on Uncle Zhang's eye and correct Wang Xiaoman's
squint. Starting at eight o'clock, she had sat on the high
operating stool for four and a half hours, concentrating under a
lamp. She had cut and stitched again and again. When she had
finished the last one and put a piece of gauze on the patient's
eye, she was stiff and her legs wouldn't move.

Having changed her clothes, Jiang called to her from the
door, 'Let's go, Wenting.'

'You go first.' She stayed where she was.

'I'll wait for you. It's my last time here.' Jiang's eyes were
watery. Was she crying? Why?

'Go on home and do your packing. Your husband must be
waiting for you.'

'He's already packed our things.' Looking up, Jiang called,
'What's wrong with your legs?'

'I've been sitting so long, they've gone to sleep! They'll be
OK in a minute. I'll come to see you this evening.'

'All right. See you then.'

After Jiang had left, Lu moved back to the wall of white tiles, supporting herself with her hands against it for a long time before going to the changing-room.

She remembered putting on her grey jacket, leaving the hospital and reaching the lane leading to her home. All of a sudden she was exhausted, more tired than she had ever felt before. The lane became long and hazy, her home seemed far away. She felt she would never get there.

She became faint. She couldn't open her eyes, her lips felt dry and stiff. She was thirsty, very thirsty. Where could she get some water?

Her parched lips trembled.

2

'Look, Dr Sun, she's come to!' Jiang cried softly. She had been sitting beside Lu all the time.

Sun Yimin, head of the Ophthalmic Department, was reading Lu's case-history and was shocked by the diagnosis of myocardial infarction. Very worried, the greying man shook his head and pushed back his black-rimmed spectacles, recalling that Lu was not the first doctor aged about forty in his department who had fallen ill with heart disease. She had been a healthy woman of forty-two. This attack was too sudden and serious.

Sun turned his tall, stooping frame to look down at Lu's pale face. She was breathing weakly, her eyes closed, her dry lips trembling slightly.

'Dr Lu,' Sun called softly.

She didn't move, her thin, puffy face expressionless.

'Wenting,' Jiang urged.

Still no reaction.

Sun raised his eyes to the forbidding oxygen cylinder, which stood in a corner of the room and then looked at the ECG monitor. He was reassured when he saw a regular QRS wave on the oscillometer. He turned back to Lu, waved his hand and said, 'Ask her husband to come in.'

A good-looking, balding man in his forties, of medium height, entered quickly. He was Fu Jiajie, Lu's husband. He had spent a sleepless night beside her and had been reluctant to leave when Sun had sent him away to lie down on the bench outside the room.

As Sun made way for him, Fu bent down to look at the familiar face, which was now so pale and strange.

Lu's lips moved again. Nobody except her husband understood her. He said, 'She wants some water. She's thirsty.'

Jiang gave him a small teapot. Carefully, Fu avoided the rubber tube leading from the oxygen cylinder and put it to Lu's parched lips. Drop by drop, the water trickled into the dying woman's mouth.

'Wenting, Wenting,' Fu called.

When a drop of water fell from Fu's shaking hand on to Lu's pallid face, the muscles seemed to twitch a little.

3

Eyes. Eyes. Eyes . . .

Many flashed past Lu's closed ones. Eyes of men and women, old and young, big and small, bright and dull, all kinds, blinking at her.

Ah! these were her husband's eyes. In them, she saw joy and sorrow, anxiety and pleasure, suffering and hope. She could see his heart through his eyes. His eyes were as bright as the golden sun in the sky. His loving heart had given her so much warmth. It was his voice, Jiajie's voice, so endearing, so gentle, and so far away, as if from another world:

> '*I wish I were a rapid stream,*
>
> . . . . . .
>
> *If my love*
> *A tiny fish would be,*
> *She'd frolic*
> *In my foaming waves.'*

Where was she? Oh, she was in a park covered with snow. There was a frozen lake, clear as crystal, on which red, blue, purple and white figures skated. Happy laughter resounded in the air while they moved arm in arm, threading their way through the crowds. She saw none of the smiling faces around her, only his. They slid on the ice, side by side, twirling, laughing. What bliss!

The ancient Five Dragon Pavilions shrouded in snow were solemn, tranquil and deserted. They leaned against the white marble balustrades, while snowflakes covered them. Holding hands tightly, they defied the severe cold.

She was young then.

She had never expected love or special happiness. Her father had deserted her mother when she was a girl, and her mother had had a hard time raising her alone. Her childhood had been bleak. All she remembered was a mother prematurely old who, night after night, sewed under a solitary lamp.

She boarded at her medical college, rising before day-break to memorize new English words, going to classes and filling scores of notebooks with neat little characters. In the evenings she studied in the library and then worked late into the night doing autopsies. She never grudged spending her youth studying.

Love had no place in her life. She shared a room with Jiang Yafen, her classmate, who had beautiful eyes, bewitching lips and who was tall, slim and lively. Every week, Jiang received love letters. Every weekend, she dated, while poor Lu did nothing, neglected by everyone.

After graduation, she and Jiang were assigned to the same hospital, which had been founded more than a hundred years earlier. Their internship lasted for four years, during which time they had to be in the hospital all day long, and remain single.

Secretly, Jiang cursed these rules, while Lu accepted the terms willingly. What did it matter being in the hospital twenty-four hours a day? She would have liked to be there forty-eight hours, if possible. No marriage for four years. Hadn't many skilled doctors married late or remained single all their lives? So she threw herself heart and soul into her work.

But life is strange. Fu Jiajie suddenly entered her quiet, routine life.

She never understood how it happened. He had been hospitalized because of an eye disease. She was his doctor.

Perhaps, his feelings for her arose from her conscientious treatment. Passionate and deep, his emotions changed both their lives.

Winter in the north is always very cold, but that winter he gave her warmth. Never having imagined love could be so intoxicating, she almost regretted not finding it earlier. She was already twenty-eight, yet she still had the heart of a young girl. With her whole being, she welcomed this late love.

> *'I wish I were a deserted forest,*
>
> *. . . . . .*
>
> *If my love*
> *A little bird would be,*
> *She'd nest and twitter*
> *In my dense trees.'*

Incredible that Fu Jiajie, whom Jiang regarded as a bookworm and who was doing research on a new material for a spacecraft in the Metallurgical Research Institute, could read poetry so well!

'Who wrote it?' Lu asked.

'The Hungarian poet Petöfi.'

'Does a scientist have time for poetry?'

'A scientist must have imagination. Science has something in common with poetry in this respect.'

Pedantic? He gave good answers.

'What about you? Do you like poetry?' he asked.

'Me? I don't know anything about it. I seldom read it.' She smiled cynically. 'The Ophthalmic Department does operations. Every stitch, every incision is strictly laid down. We can't use the slightest imagination . . .'

Fu cut in, 'Your work is a beautiful poem. You can make many people see again . . .'

Smiling, he moved over to her, his face close to hers. His masculinity, which she had never experienced before, assailed, bewildered and unnerved her. She felt something must happen, and, sure enough, he put his arms round her, embracing her tightly.

It had occurred so suddenly that she looked fearfully at the smiling eyes close to hers and his parted lips. Her heart thumping, her head raised, she closed her eyes in embarrassment, moving away instinctively as his irrestible love flooded her.

Beihai Park in the snow was just the right place for her. Snow covered the tall dagoba, Qiongdao Islet with its green pines, the long corridor and quiet lake. It also hid the sweet shyness of the lovers.

To everyone's surprise, after her four-year internship had ended, Lu was the first to get married. Fate had decided Fu Jiajie's intrusion. How could she refuse his wish that they marry? How insistently and strongly he wanted her, preparing to sacrifice everything for her! . . .

> *'I wish I were a crumbling ruin,*
> *. . . . . .*
> *If my love*
> *Green ivy would be,*
> *She'd tenderly entwine*
> *Around my lonely head.'*

Life was good, love was beautiful. These recollections gave her strength, and her eyelids opened slightly.

4

After heavy dosages of sedatives and analgesics Dr Lu was still in a coma. The head of the Internal Medicine Department gave her a careful examination, studied her ECG and her case-history, then told the ward doctor to keep up the intravenous drip and injections of opiate and morphine and to watch out for changes in her ECG monitor to guard against more serious complications due to the myocardial infarction.

On leaving the ward he remarked to Sun, 'She's too weak. I remember how fit Dr Lu was when she first came here.'

'Yes.' Sun shook his head with a sigh. 'It's eighteen years since she came to our hospital, just a girl.'

Eighteen years ago Dr Sun had already been a well-known ophthalmologist, respected by all his colleagues for his skill and responsible attitude to work. This able, energetic professor in his prime regarded it as his duty to train the younger doctors. Each time the medical college assigned them a new batch of graduates, he examined them one by one to make his choice. He thought the first step to making their Ophthalmology Department the best in all China was by selecting the most promising interns.

How had he chosen Lu? He remembered quite distinctly. At first this twenty-four-year-old graduate had not made much of an impression on him.

That morning Department Head Sun had already interviewed five of the graduates assigned to them and had been most disappointed. Some of them were suitable, but they were not interested in the Ophthalmology Department and did not want to work there. Others wanted to be oculists because they thought it a simple, easy job. By the time he picked up the sixth file marked Lu Wenting, he was rather tired and not expecting much. He was reflecting that the medical college's teaching needed improving to give students a correct impression from the start of his department.

The door opened quietly. A slim girl walked softly in. Looking up he saw that she had on a cotton jacket and slacks. Her cuffs were patched, the knees of her blue slacks were faded. Simply dressed, she was even rather shabby. He read the name on her file, then glanced at her casually. She really looked like a little girl, slightly built, with an oval face and neatly bobbed glossy black hair. She calmly sat down on the chair facing him.

Asked the usual technical questions, she answered each in turn, saying no more than was strictly necessary.

'You want to work in the Ophthalmology Department?' Sun asked lethargically, having almost decided to wind up this interview. His elbows on the desk, he rubbed his temples with his fingers.

'Yes. At college I was interested in ophthalmology.' She spoke with a slight southern accent.

Delighted by this answer. Sun lowered his hands as if his head no longer ached. He had changed his mind. Watching her carefully he asked more seriously, 'What aroused your interest?'

At once this question struck him as inappropriate, too hard to answer. But she replied confidently, 'Ophthalmology is lagging behind in our country.'

'Good, tell me in what way it's backward,' he asked eagerly.

'I don't know how to put it, but I feel we haven't tried out certain operations which are done abroad. Such as using laser beams to seal retina wounds. I think we ought to try these methods too.'

'Right!' Mentally, Sun had already given her full marks. 'What else? Any other ideas?'

'Yes . . . well . . . making more use of freezing to remove cataracts. Anyway, it seems to me there are many new problems that ought to be studied.'

'Good, that makes sense. Can you read foreign materials?'

'With difficulty, using a dictionary. I like foreign languages.'

'Excellent.'

That was the first time Sun had praised a new student like this to her face. A few days later Lu Wenting and Jiang Yafen were the first to be admitted to his department. Sun chose Jiang for her intelligence, enthusiasm and enterprise, Lu for her simplicity, seriousness and keenness.

The first year they performed external ocular operations and studied ophthalmology. The second year they operated on eyeballs and studied ophthalmometry and ophthalmomyology. By the third year they were able to do such tricky operations as those for cataract. That year something happened which made Sun see Lu in a new light.

It was a spring morning, a Monday. Sun made his round of the wards followed by white-coated doctors, some senior, some junior. The patients were sitting up in bed expectantly, hoping this famous professor would examine their eyes, as if with one touch of his hand he could heal them.

Each time he came to a bed, Sun picked up the case-history hanging behind it and read it while listening to the attending oculist or some senior oculist report on the diagnosis and treatment. Sometimes he raised a patient's eyelid to look at his eye, sometimes patted him on the shoulder and urged him not to worry about his operation, then moved on to the next bed.

After the ward round they held a short consultation, at which tasks were assigned. It was generally Dr Sun and the attending oculists who spoke, while the residents listened carefully, not venturing to speak for fear of making fools of themselves in front of these authorities. Today was the same. All that had to be said had been said and tasks were assigned. As he stood up to leave, Sun asked, 'Have the rest of you anything to add?'

A girl spoke up in a low voice from one corner of the room, 'Dr Sun, will you please have another look at the X-ray of the patient in Bed 3 Ward 4?'

All heads turned in her direction. Sun saw that the speaker was Lu. She was so short, so inconspicuous, that he had not noticed her following him in the wards. Back in the office where they had talked at some length, he had still not noticed her presence.

'Bed 3?' he turned to the chief resident.

'An industrial accident,' he was told.

'When he was admitted to hospital an X-ray was taken of his eye,' Lu said. 'The radiologist's report said there was no sign of a metal foreign body. After hospitalization the wound was sewn up and healed, but the patient complained of pain. I had another X-ray taken, and I believe there really is a foreign body. Will you have a look, Dr Sun?'

The film was fetched. Sun examined it. The chief resident and attending oculists then passed it round.

Jiang looked wide-eyed at her classmate, thinking, 'Couldn't you have waited until after the meeting to ask Dr Sun to look at that? If by any chance you're wrong, the whole department will gossip. Even if you're right, you're implying that the doctors in the Outpatients Department are careless, and they are attending oculists!'

'You're right, there's a foreign body.' Sun took back the picture and nodded. Looking round at the others he said, 'Dr Lu has not been long in our department. Her careful, responsible attitude is admirable, and so is her hard study.'

Lu lowered her head. This unexpected praise in public made

her blush. At sight of this Sun smiled. He knew it took great courage and a strong sense of responsibility for a resident oculist to challenge an attending one's diagnosis.

Hospitals have a more complex hierarchy than other organizations. It was an unwritten rule that junior doctors should defer to their seniors; residents should obey the attending doctors; and there could be no disputing the opinions of professors and associate professors. So Sun attached special importance to Lu's query, since she was so very junior.

From then on his estimate of Lu was, 'She's a very promising oculist.'

Now eighteen years had passed. Lu, Jiang and their age group had become the backbone of his department. If promotion had been based on competence, they should long ago have had the rank of department heads. But this had not happened, and they were still not even attending doctors. For eighteen years their status had been that of interns, for the 'cultural revolution' had broken the ladder leading to promotion.

The sight of Lu at her last gasp filled him with compassion. He stopped the head of the Internal Medicine Department to ask, 'What do you think? Will she pull through?'

The department head looked towards her ward and sighed, then shook his head and said softly, 'Old Sun, we can only hope she'll soon be out of danger.'

Sun walked back anxiously to the ward. His steps were heavy, he was showing his age. From the doorway he saw Jiang still beside Lu's pillow. He halted, not wanting to disturb the two close friends.

In late autumn the nights are long. Darkness fell before six. The soughing wind rustled the phoenix trees outside the window. One by one their withered yellow leaves were blown away.

Sun, watching the whirling yellow leaves outside and listening to the wind, felt gloomier than before. Here were two skilled ophthalmologists, two key members of his staff, one had collapsed and might never recover, the other was leaving and might never return. They were two of the mainstays of his department in this prestigious hospital. Without them, he felt his department would be like the phoenix trees buffeted by the wind. It would deteriorate from day to day.

5

She seemed to be walking along an endless road, not a winding mountain path which urged people on, nor a narrow one between fields of fragrant rice. This was a desert, a quagmire, a wasteland, devoid of people and silent. Walking was difficult and exhausting.

Lie down and rest. The desert was warm, the quagmire soft. Let the ground warm her rigid body, the sunshine caress her tired limbs. Death was calling softly, 'Rest, Dr Lu!'

Lie down and rest. Everlasting rest. No thoughts, feelings, worries, sadness or exhaustion.

But she couldn't do that. At the end of the long road, her patients were waiting for her. She seemed to see one patient tossing and turning in bed with the pain in his eyes, crying quietly at the threat of blindness. She saw many eager eyes waiting for her. She heard her patients calling to her in despair, 'Dr Lu!'

This was a sacred call, an irresistible one. She trudged along the long road dragging her numb legs, from her home to the hospital, from the clinic to the ward, from one village to another with a medical team. Day by day, month by month, year by year, she trudged on . . .

'Dr Lu!'

Who was calling? Director Zhao? Yes. He had called her by phone. She remembered putting down the receiver, handing over her patient to Jiang, who shared her consulting-room, and heading for the director's office.

She hurried through a small garden, ignoring the white and yellow chrysanthemums, the fragrance of the osmanthus and the fluttering butterflies. She wanted to quickly finish her business with Zhao and return to her patients. There were seventeen waiting that morning, and she had only seen seven so far. Tomorrow she was on ward duty. She wanted to make arrangements for some of the out-patients.

She remembered not knocking but walking straight in. A man and woman were sitting on the sofa. She halted. Then she saw Director Zhao in his swivel-chair.

'Come in please, Dr Lu,' Zhao greeted her.

She walked over and sat down on a leather chair by the window.

The large room was bright, tidy and quiet, unlike the noisy clinic, where sometimes the children howled. She felt odd, unused to the quietness and cleanliness of the room.

The couple looked cultured and composed. Director Zhao was always erect and scholarly looking, with well-groomed hair, a kind face and smiling eyes behind gold-rimmed spectacles. He had on a white shirt, a well-pressed light grey suit and shining black leather shoes.

The man sitting on the sofa was tall and greying at the temples. A pair of sun-glasses shielded his eyes. Lu saw at a glance that he had eye trouble. Leaning back against the sofa, he was playing with his walking-stick.

The woman in her fifties was still attractive, despite her age. Though her hair was dyed and permed, it did not look cheap. Her clothes were well-cut and expensive.

Lu remembered how the woman had sized her up, following her about with her eyes. Her face showed doubt, uneasiness and disappointment.

'Dr Lu, let me introduce you to Vice-minister Jiao Chengsi and his wife Comrade Qin Bo.'

A vice-minister? Well, in the past ten years and more, she had treated many ministers, Party secretaries and directors. She had never paid attention to titles. She simply wondered what was wrong with his eyes. Was he losing his sight?

Director Zhao asked, 'Dr Lu, are you in the clinic or on duty in the ward?'

'Starting from tomorrow, I'll be on ward duty.'

'Fine,' he laughed. 'Vice-minister Jiao wants to have his cataract removed.'

That meant she was given the task. She asked the man, 'Is it one eye?'

'Yes.'

'Which one?'

'The left one.'

'Can't you see with it at all?'

The patient shook his head.

'Did you see a doctor before?'

As she rose to examine his eye, she remembered he named a hospital. Then his wife, who was sitting beside him, politely stopped her.

'There's no hurry, Dr Lu. Sit down, please. We ought to go to your clinic for an examination.' Smiling, Qin Bo turned to Director Zhao. 'Since he developed eye trouble, I've become something of an oculist myself.'

Though Lu didn't examine him, she stayed a long time. What had they talked about? Qin had asked her many personal questions.

'How long have you been here, Dr Lu?'

She hadn't kept track of the years. She only remembered the year she had graduated. So she answered, 'I came here in 1961.'

'Eighteen years ago.' Qin counted on her fingers.

Why was she so interested in this? Then Director Zhao chipped in, 'Dr Lu has a lot of experience. She's a skilled surgeon.'

Qin went on, 'You don't seem to be in good health, Dr Lu.'

What was she driving at? Lu was so busy caring for others, that she had never given any thought to her own health. The hospital didn't even have her case-history. And none of her leaders had ever inquired after her health. Why was this stranger showing such concern? She hesitated before answering, 'I'm very well.'

Zhao added again, 'She's one of the fittest. Dr Lu's never missed a day's work for years.'

Lu made no answer, wondering why this was so important to this lady, and fretting to get back to her patients. Jiang couldn't possibly cope with so many alone.

Her eyes fixed on Lu, the lady smiled and pressed, 'Are you sure you can remove a cataract easily, Dr Lu?'

Another difficult question. She had had no accidents so far, but anything could happen if the patient didn't co-operate well or if the anaesthetic was not carefully applied.

She couldn't recollect whether she had made a reply, only Qin's big eyes staring at her with doubt, unsettling her. Having treated all kinds of patients, she had got used to the difficult wives of high cadres. She was searching for a tactful answer when Jiao moved impatiently and turned his head to his wife, who stopped and averted her gaze.

How had this trying conversation finished? Oh, yes, Jiang had come to tell her that Uncle Zhang had come for his appointment.

Qin quickly said politely, 'You can go, Dr Lu, if you're busy.'

Lu left the big bright room, which was so suffocating. She could hardly breathe.

She was suffocating.

6

Shortly before the day ended, Director Zhao hurried over to the internal medicine ward.

'Dr Lu's always enjoyed good health, Dr Sun. Why should she have this sudden attack?' his hands in his pockets, Zhao asked Sun as they headed for Lu's ward. Eight years Sun's junior, Zhao looked much younger, his voice more powerful.

He shook his head and went on, 'This is a warning. Middle-aged doctors are the backbone of our hospital. Their heavy responsiblities and daily chores are ruining their health. If they collapse one by one, we'll be in a fix. How many people are there in her family? How many rooms does she have?'

Looking at Sun, who was depressed and worried, he added, 'What? . . . four in a room? So that's how it is! What's her wage? . . . 56.50 yuan! That's why people say better to be a barber with a razor than a surgeon with a scalpel. There's some truth in it. Right? Why wasn't her salary raised last year?'

'There were too many. You can't raise everyone's,' Sun said cynically.

'I hope you'll talk that problem over with the Party branch. Ask them to investigate the work, income and living conditions of the middle-aged doctors and send me a report.'

'What's the use of that? A similar report was sent in in 1978,' Sun retorted politely, his eyes on the ground.

'Stop grumbling, Dr Sun. A report's better than nothing. I can show it to the municipal Party committee, the Ministry of Health and whomever it concerns. The Party Central Committee has stressed time and again that talented people and intellectuals should be valued and their salaries increased. We can't ignore it. The day before yesterday, at a meeting of the municipal committee, it was stressed that attention should be paid to middle-aged personnel. I believe their problems will be solved.' Zhao stopped when they entered Lu's room.

Fu Jiajie stood up as Zhao entered. He waved his hand in greeting and walked over to Lu, bent down and examined her face. Then he took her case-history from her doctor. From a director he had turned into a doctor.

Zhao, a noted thorax expert, had returned to China after Liberation. Very enthusiastic politically, he was praised for both his political consciousness and his medical skill, joining the Party in the fifties. When later he was made director, he had to take part in so many meetings and do so much administrative work, that he seldom found the opportunity to see patients except for important consultations. During the 'cultural revolution', he had been detained illegally and made to sweep the hospital grounds. The last three years, as director again, he had been so tied up with daily problems that he practically had no time or energy for surgery.

Now he had come specially to see Lu. All the ward doctors had gathered behind him.

But he didn't say anything startling. Having read the case-history and looked at the ECG monitor, he told the doctors to note any changes and watch out for complications. Then he asked, 'Is her husband here?'

Sun introduced Fu. Zhao wondered why this charming man in his prime was already going bald. Apparently, a man who couldn't look after himself couldn't look after his wife.

'It won't be easy,' Zhao told him. 'She needs complete rest. She'll need help for everything, even to turn over in bed. Help twenty-four hours a day. Where do you work? You'll have to ask for leave. You can't do it all by yourself either. Is there anyone else in your family?'

Fu shook his head. 'Just two small children.'

Zhao turned to Sun, 'Can you spare someone from your department?'

'For one or two days, maybe.'

'That'll do to begin with.'

His eyes returning to Lu's thin pale face, Zhao still couldn't understand why this energetic woman had suddenly collapsed.

It occurred to him that she might have been too nervous operating on Vice-minister Jiao. Then he dismissed the thought. She was experienced and it was highly improbable that an attack had been brought on by nervousness. Besides, myocardial infarction often had no obvious cause.

But he couldn't dismiss the notion that there was some kind of a link between Jiao's operation and Lu's illness. He regretted having recommended her. In fact, Jiao's wife, Qin Bo, had been reluctant to have her right from the beginning.

That day, after Lu's departure, Qin had asked, 'Director Zhao, is Dr Lu the vice-head of her department?'

'No.'

'Is she an attending doctor?'

'No.'

'Is she a Party member?'

'No.'

Qin said bluntly, 'Excuse my outspokenness since we're all Party members, but I think it's rather inappropriate to let an ordinary doctor operate on Vice-minister Jiao.'

Jiao stopped her by banging his walking-stick on the floor. Turning to her he said angrily, 'What are you talking about, Qin Bo? Let the hospital make the arrangements. Any surgeon can operate.'

Qin retorted heatedly, 'That's not the right attitude, Old Jiao. You must be responsible. You can work only if you're healthy. We must be responsible to the revolution and the Party.'

Zhao quickly butted in to avoid a quarrel, 'Believe me, Comrade Qin, although she's not a Communist, Lu's a good doctor. And she's very good at removing cataracts. Don't worry!'

'It's not that, Director Zhao. And I'm not being too careful either.' Qin sighed, 'When I was in the cadre school, one old comrade had to have that operation. He was not allowed to come back to Beijing. So he went to a small hospital there. Before the operation was through his eyeball fell out. Jiao was detained by the followers of the gang for seven years! He has just resumed work. He can't do without his eyes.'

'Nothing like that will happen, Comrade Qin. We have very few accidents in our hospital.'

Qin still tried to argue her point. 'Can we ask Dr Sun, the department head, to operate on Jiao?

Zhao shook his head and laughed. 'Dr Sun's almost seventy and has poor eyesight himself! Besides, he hasn't operated for years. He does research, advises the younger doctors and teaches. Dr Lu's a better surgeon than he.'

'How about Dr Guo then?'

Zhao stared. 'Dr Guo?' She must have made a thorough investigation of the department.

She prompted, 'Guo Ruqing.'

Zhao gestured helplessly. 'He's left the country.'

Qin wouldn't give up. 'When is he coming back?'

'He's not.'

'What do you mean?' This time she stared.

Zhao sighed. 'Dr Guo's wife returned from abroad. When her father, a shopkeeper, died, he left his store to them. So they decided to leave.'

'To leave medicine for a store? I can't understand it.' Jiao sighed too.

'He's not the only one. Several of our capable doctors have left or are preparing to go.'

Qin was indignant. 'I don't understand their mentality.'

Jiao waved his stick and turned to Zhao, 'In the early fifties, intellectuals like you overcame many difficulties to return here to help build a new China. But now, the intellectuals we've trained are leaving the country. It's a serious lesson.'

'This can't go on,' said Qin. 'We must do more ideological work. After the gang was smashed, the social status of intellectuals was raised a lot. Their living and working conditions will improve as China modernizes.'

'Yes. Our Party committee holds the same view. I talked with Dr Guo twice on behalf of the Party and begged him to stay. But it was no use.'

Qin, who was about to continue, was stopped by Jiao who said, 'Director Zhao, I didn't come to insist on having an expert or a professor. I came because I have confidence in your hospital, or to be exact, because I have a special feeling for your hospital. A few years ago, the cataract in my right eye was removed here. And it was superbly done.'

'Who did it?' Zhao asked.

Jiao answered sadly, 'I never found out who she was.'

'That's easy. We can look up your case-history.'

Zhao picked up the receiver, thinking that Qin would be satisfied if he got that doctor. But Jiao stopped him. 'You can't find her. I had it done as an out-patient. There was no case-history. It was a woman with a southern accent.'

'That's difficult.' Zhao laughed, replacing the receiver. 'We have many women doctors who speak with a southern accent. Dr Lu also comes from the south. Let her do it.'

The couple agreed. Qin helped Jiao up and they left.

Was this the cause of Lu's illness? Zhao couldn't believe it. She had performed this operation hundreds of times. She wouldn't be so nervous. He had gone over before the operation and found her confident, composed and well. Why this sudden attack, then?

Zhao looked again at Lu with concern. Even on the brink of death, she looked as if she were sleeping peacefully.

7

Lu was always composed, quiet and never flustered. Another

woman would have retorted or shown her indignation at Qin's insulting questions or, at the very least, felt resentful afterwards. But Lu had left Zhao's office as calm as ever, neither honoured to be chosen to operate on Vice-minister Jiao nor humiliated by Qin's questions. The patient had the right to decide whether or not he wanted an operation. That was all there was to it.

'Well, what big official wants you this time?' Jiang asked softly.

'It's not definite yet.'

'Let's hurry.' Jiang steered her along. 'I couldn't persuade your Uncle Zhang. He's made up his mind not to have the operation.'

'That's nonsense! He travelled a long way to get here and spent much money. He'll be able to see after the transplant. It's our duty to cure him.'

'Then you talk him round.'

Passing by the waiting room, they smiled and nodded at the familiar patients who stood up to greet them. Back in her room, while Lu was seeing a young man, she was interrupted by a voice booming, 'Dr Lu!'

Both Lu and her patient looked up as a tall sturdy man advanced. In his fifties, he was broad-shouldered, wearing black trousers and a shirt and a white towel round his head. At his cry, the people in the corridor quickly made way for him. A head above everyone else and almost blind, he was unaware that he attracted so much attention as he groped his way in the direction of Lu's voice.

Lu hurried forward to help him. 'Sit down, please, Uncle Zhang.'

'Thank you, Dr Lu. I want to tell you something.'

'Yes, but sit down first.' Lu helped him to a chair.

'I've been in Beijing quite a while now. I'm thinking of going home tomorrow and coming back some other time.'

'I don't agree. You've come such a long way and spent so much money . . .'

'That's just it,' Uncle Zhang cut in, slapping his thigh. 'So I think I'll go home, do some work and earn some more workpoints. Although I can't see, I can still do some work and the brigade's very kind to me. I've made up my mind to leave, Dr Lu. But I couldn't go without saying goodbye to you. You've done so much for me.'

Having suffered from corneal ulcers for many years, he had come to the hospital to have a transplant, a suggestion proposed by Lu when she had visited his brigade with a medical team.

'Your son spent a lot of money to send you here, We can't let you go home like this.'

'I feel better already!'

Lu laughed. 'When you're cured, you can work for another twenty years since you're so strong.'

Uncle Zhang laughed. 'You bet I will! I can do anything if my eyes are good.'

'Then stay and have them treated.'

Zhang confided, 'Listen, Dr Lu, I'll tell you the truth. I'm worried about money. I can't afford to live in a Beijing hotel.'

Stunned, Lu quickly told him, 'I know you're next on the list. Once there's a donor, it'll be your turn.'

He finally agreed to stay. Lu helped him out. Then a little girl of eleven accosted her.

Her pretty, rosy face was marred by a squint. Dressed in hospital pyjamas, she called timidly, 'Dr Lu.'

'Why don't you stay in the ward, Wang Xiaoman?' She had been admitted the previous day.

'I'm scared. I want to go home.' She began to cry. 'I don't want an operation.'

Lu put one arm around her. 'Tell me why you don't want an operation.'

'It'll hurt too much.'

'It won't, you silly girl! I'll give you an anaesthetic. It won't hurt at all.' Lu patted her head and bent down to look with regret at the damaged work of art. She said, 'Look, won't it be nice when I make this eye look like the other one? Now go back to your ward. You mustn't run around in a hospital.

When the little girl had wiped away her tears and left, Lu returned to her patients.

There had been many patients the last few days. She must make up for the time she had lost in Zhao's office. Forgetting Jiao, Qin and herself, she saw one patient after another.

A nurse came to tell her she was wanted on the phone.

Lu excused herself.

It was the kindergarten nurse informing her, 'Xiaojia has a temperature. It started last night. I know you're busy, so I took her to the doctor, who gave her an injection. She's still feverish and is asking for you. Can you come?'

'I'll be there in a minute.' She replaced the receiver.

But she couldn't go immediately since many patients were waiting. She rang her husband, but was told that he had gone out to a meeting.

Back in her office, Jiang asked, 'Who called? Anything important?'

'Nothing.'

Lu never troubled others, not even her leaders. 'I'll go to the kindergarten when I'm through with the patients,' she thought as she returned to her desk. At first she imagined her daughter crying and calling her. Later she saw only the patients' eyes. She hurried to the kindergarten when she had finished.

8

'Why did it take so long?' the nurse complained.

Lu walked quickly to the isolation room where her little daughter lay, her face flushed with fever, her lips parted, her eyes closed, her breathing difficult.

She bent over the crib. 'Mummy's here, darling.'

Xiaojia moved and called in a hoarse voice, 'Mummy, let's go home.'

'All right, my pet.'

She first took Xiaojia to her own hospital to see a pediatrician. 'It's pneumonia,' the sympathetic doctor told her. 'You must take good care of her.'

She nodded and left after Xiaojia had been given an injection and some medicine.

In the hospital everything stood still at noon, the outpatients having left, the inpatients sleeping and the hospital staff resting. The spacious grounds were deserted except for the chirping sparrows flying among the trees. Nature still competed with men in this noisy centre of the city, where tall buildings rose compactly and the air was polluted. In the hospital all day, Lu had never been aware of the birds before.

She couldn't make up her mind where to take her daughter, hating to leave the sick child alone in the kindergarten's isolation room. But who could look after her at home?

After some hesitation she steeled herself and headed for the kindergarten.

'No. I don't want to go there,' Xiaojia wailed on her shoulder.

'Be a good girl, Xiaojia . . .'

'No. I want to go home!' She began kicking.

'All right. We'll go home.'

They had to go along a busy street with recently pasted advertisements of the latest fashions. Lu never so much as glanced at the costly goods in the shopwindows, or the produce the peasants sold in the streets. With two children, it was hard to make ends meet. Now, carrying Xiaojia in her arms amd worrying about Yuanyuan at home, she was even less eager to look around.

Arriving home at one o'clock, Lu found a pouting Yuanyuan waiting for her. 'Why are you so late, Mummy?' he asked.

'Xiaojia's ill,' Lu answered curtly, putting Xiaojia on the bed, undressing her and tucking her in.

Standing at the table Yuanyuan fretted, 'Please cook lunch, Mummy. I'll be late.'

In frustration, Lu shouted at him, 'You'll drive me crazy if you go on like that!'

Wronged and in a hurry, Yuanyuan was on the point of tears. Ignoring him, Lu went to stoke up the fire, which had almost gone out. The pots and the cupboard were empty. There were no left-overs from yesterday's meals.

She went back into the room, reproaching herself for having been so harsh on the poor boy.

In the past few years, keeping house had become an increasing burden. During the 'cultural revolution' her husband's laboratory had been closed down and his research project scrapped. All he had needed to do was to show his face in the office for an hour in the morning and afternoon. He spent the remainder of his day and talents on domestic chores, cooking and learning to sew and knit, lifting the burden entirely from Lu's shoulders. After the gang was smashed, scientific research was resumed and Fu, a capable metallurgist, was busy again. Most of the housework was shouldered once more by Lu.

Every day at noon, she went home to cook. It was an effort to stoke up the fire, prepare the vegetables and be ready to serve the meal in fifty minutes so that Yuanyuan, Fu and herself could return to school or work on time.

When anything unexpected cropped up, the whole family went hungry. She sighed and gave her son some money. 'Go and buy yourself a bun, Yuanyuan.'

He turned back half-way, 'What about you, Mummy?'

'I'm not hungry.'

'I'll buy you a bun too.'

Yuanyuan soon came home with two buns and gave one to his mother. He left for school immediately, eating his on the way.

Biting into the cold hard bun, Lu looked around at her small room, which was twelve metres square.

She and her husband had been content with a simple life, living in this room since their marriage, without a sofa, wardrobe or a new desk. They had the same furniture they had used when they were single.

Though they owned few material possessions, they had many books. Aunt Chen, a neighbour, had commented, 'What will the two bookworms live on?' But they were happy. All they had wanted was a small room, some clothes, and three simple meals a day.

Treasuring their time, they put their evenings to good use. Every night, when their neighbours' naughty children peeped into their small room to spy on the new couple, they invariably found them at work: Lu occupying their only desk studying foreign material with the help of a dictionary and taking notes, while Fu read reference books on a stack of chests.

The evening was not wasted when they could study late quietly and undisturbed. In the summer, their neighbours sat cooling themselves in the courtyard, but the smell of tea, the light breeze, bright stars, interesting news and conversation . . . none of these could lure them from their stuffy little room.

Their quiet life and studious evenings ended much too soon. Lu gave birth to Yuanyuan and then to Xiaojia. Their lovely children brought disorder and hardship as well as joy to their lives. When the crib was later replaced by a single bed and the tiny room filled with children's clothes, pots and pans, they could hardly move about. Peace was shattered by their children laughing and crying.

What could an oculist achieve without keeping up with foreign developments in the field? Therefore, Lu often sat reading behind a curtain in the room late into the night.

When Yuanyuan began school he had to use their only desk. Only when he had finished doing his home-work was it Lu's turn to spread out her notebook and the medical books she had borrowed. Fu came last.

How hard life was!

Lu fixed her eyes on the little clock: One five, one ten, one fifteen. Time to go to work. What should she do? Lots of things needed winding up before she went to the ward tomorrow. What about Xiaojia? Should she call her husband? There was no telephone booth near by and, anyway, she probably could not get him. As he had wasted ten years, better not disturb him.

She frowned, at a loss what to do.

Perhaps she shouldn't have married. Some claimed that marriage ended love. She had naively believed that, though it might be true for some, it could not happen to her. If she had been more prudent, she would not have been weighed down by the burdens of marriage and a family.

One twenty. She must turn to her neighbour Aunt Chen, a kind-hearted woman who had helped on many occasions . . . Since she would not accept anything for her services, Lu was reluctant to trouble her.

Still she had to this time. Aunt Chen was most obliging,

'Leave her to me, Dr Lu.'

Lu put some children's books and building blocks beside Xiaojia, asked Aunt Chen to give her the medicine and hurried to the hospital.

She had intended to tell the nurse not to send her too many patients so that she could go home early, but once she started work, she forgot everything.

Zhao called her up to remind her that Jiao was to be admitted the following day.

Qin called twice asking about the operation and how Jiao and his family should prepare mentally and materially.

Lu was hard put to it to give an answer. She had performed hundreds of such operations and no one had ever asked her that before. So she said, 'Oh, nothing special.'

'Really? But surely it's better to be well prepared. What if I come over and we have a chat?'

Lu quickly told her, 'I'm busy this afternoon.'

'Then we'll talk tomorrow in the hospital.'

'OK.'

When the trying conversation had ended, Lu had returned to her office. It was dark before she had finished her clinic.

Arriving home she heard Aunt Chen singing an impromptu song:

> 'Grow up, my dear,
> To be an engineer.'

Xiaojia laughed happily. Lu thanked Aunt Chen and was relieved to find Xiaojia's temperature down.

She gave her an injection. After Fu returned, Jiang Yafen and her husband, Liu, called.

'We've come to say goodbye,' said Jiang.

'Where are you going?' Lu inquired.

'We've just got our visas for Canada,' replied Jiang, her eyes fixed on the ground.

Liu's father, a doctor in Canada, had urged them to join him there. Lu had not expected them to go.

'How long will you stay? When will you come back?' she asked.

'Maybe for good.' Liu shrugged his shoulders.

'Why didn't you let me know earlier, Yafen?' Lu turned to her friend.

'I was afraid that you'd try to stop me. I was afraid I'd change my mind.' Jiang avoided her eyes, staring hard at the ground.

From his bag, Liu produced some wine and food and said in high spirits, 'I bet you haven't cooked yet. Let's have our farewell banquet here.'

9

It was a sorrowful farewell party that evening.

They seemed to be drinking tears instead of wine. To be tasting the bitterness of life instead of delicious dishes.

Xiaojia was asleep, Yuanyuan watching TV next door. Liu raised his cup, eyeing the wine in it, and said with feeling, 'Life—it's hard to tell how life will turn out! My father was a doctor with a sound classical education. As a child I loved old poetry and longed to become a writer, but I was fated to follow in his footsteps, and now over thirty years have gone. My father was extremely circumspect. His maxim was "Too much talk leads to trouble." Unfortunately I didn't take after him. I like talking and airing my views, so that landed me in trouble and I got bashed in each political movement. When I graduated in '57, I missed being labelled a Rightist by the skin of my teeth. In the "cultural revolution", it goes without saying, I was flayed. I'm Chinese. I can't claim to have high political consciousness, but at least I love my country and really want China to become rich and strong. I never dreamed that now that I'm nearing fifty I'd suddenly leave my homeland.'

'Do you really have to go?' Lu asked gently.

'Yes. Why? I've debated this with myself many times.' Liu shook the half-full cup of red wine he was holding. 'I've passed middle age and may not live many years longer. Why should I leave my ashes in a strange land?'

The others listened in silence to this expression of his grief at leaving. Now he suddenly broke off, drained his cup and blurted out, 'Go on, curse me! I'm China's unfilial son!'

'Don't say that, Liu. We all know what you've been through.' Fu refilled his cup. 'Now those dark years are over, the sun is shining again. Everything will change for the better.'

'I believe that.' Liu nodded. 'But when will the sun shine on our family? Shine on our daughter? I can't wait.'

'Let's not talk about that.' Lu guessed that Liu felt impelled to leave for the sake of his only daughter. Not wanting to go into this, she changed the subject. 'I never drink, but today before you and Yafen leave I want to drink to you.'

'No, we should drink to *you*.' Liu put down his cup. 'You're the mainstay of our hospital, one of China's up-and-coming doctors!'

'You're drunk,' she laughed.

'I'm not.'

Jiang, who had been keeping quiet, now raised her cup and said, 'I drink to you from the bottom of my heart! To our twenty-odd years of friendship, and to our future eye-specialist!'

'Goodness! You're talking nonsense! Who am I?' Lu brushed aside this compliment.

'Who are you?' Liu was really half tipsy. 'You live in cramped quarters and slave away regardless of criticism, not seeking fame or money. A hard-working doctor like you is an ox serving the children, as Lu Xun said, eating grass and providing milk. Isn't that right, Old Fu?'

Fu drank in silence and nodded.

'There are many people like that, I'm not the only one,' Lu demurred with a smile.

'That's why ours is a great nation!' Liu drained another cup.

Jiang glanced at Xiaojia sound asleep on the bed, and said sympathetically, 'Yes, you're too busy attending to your patients to nurse your own little girl.'

Liu stood up to fill all the cups and declared, 'She's sacrificing herself to save mankind.'

'What's come over you today, boosting me like this?' Lu wagged a finger at Fu. 'You ask him if I'm not selfish, driving my husband into the kitchen and turning my children into ragamuffins. I've messed up the whole family. The fact is, I'm neither a good wife nor mother.'

'You're a good doctor!' Liu cried.

Fu took another sip of wine, then put down his cup and commented, 'I think your hospital is to blame. Doctors have homes and children like everyone else. And their children may fall ill. Why does no one show any consideration for them?'

'Fu!' Liu cut in loudly. 'If I were Director Zhao, I'd first give you a medal, and one each to Yuanyuan and Xiaojia. You're the ones victimized to provide our hospital with such a fine doctor . . '

Fu interrupted, 'I don't want a medal or a citation. I just wish your hospital understood how hard it is to be a doctor's husband. As soon as the order comes to go out on medical tours or relief work, she's up and off, leaving the family. She comes back so exhausted from the operating theatre, she can't raise a finger to cook a meal. That being the case, if I don't go into the kitchen, who will? I should really be grateful to the "cultural revolution" for giving me all that time to learn to cook.'

'Yafen said long ago that your "bookworm" label should be torn off.' Liu patted his shoulder and laughed. 'You can study one of the most advanced branches of science for space travel, and put on a stunning performance in the kitchen—you're becoming one of the new men of the communist era. Who says the "cultural revolution's" achievements were not the main aspect of it?'

Fu normally never drank. Today after a few cups his face was red. He caught hold of Liu's sleeve and chuckled, 'Right, the "cultural revolution" was a great revolution to remould us. Didn't those few years change me into a male housewife? If you don't believe it, ask Wenting. Didn't I turn my hand to every chore?'

This embittered joking upset Lu. But she could not stop them. It seemed this was now the only way to lessen their grief at parting. She forced herself to smile back at her husband.

'You learned to do everything except sew cloth shoe-soles. That's why Yuanyuan keeps clamouring for a pair of gymshoes.'

'You expect too much,' said Liu with a straight face.

'However thoroughly Fu remoulds himself, he can't turn into an old village woman carrying a shoe-sole around everywhere!'

'If the "gang of four" hadn't been smashed, I might really have carried a shoe-sole to the criticism meetings in my institute,' said Fu. 'Just think, if things had gone on like that, science, technology and learning would all have been scrapped, leaving nothing but sewing cloth shoe-soles.'

But how long could they keep up these wry jokes? They talked of the springtime of science since the overthrow of the gang, of the improved political status of intellectuals although they were underpaid, of the difficulties of middle-aged professionals. The atmosphere became heavy again.

'Old Liu, you have lots of contacts, it's too bad you're leaving.' Fu roused himself to slap Liu on the back. 'I hear home helps are well paid. I'd like you to find me a place as a domestic.'

'My leaving doesn't matter,' Liu retorted. 'Just put an ad in that new paper *The Market*.'

'That's a good idea!' Fu adjusted his thick-rimmed glasses. 'The advertiser is a university graduate with a mastery of two foreign languages. A good cook, tailor and washerman, able to do both skilled and heavy work. His health is sound, his temper good, he's bold, hard-working and willing to accept criticism. And, last of all, his wages can be settled at the interview.' He laughed.

Jiang was sitting quietly, neither eating nor drinking. Watching them laugh, she wanted to join in but could not. She nudged her husband.

'Don't talk like that, what's the point?'

'This is a widespread social phenomenon, that's the point.' Liu made a sweeping gesture. 'Middle age, middle age. Everyone agrees that middle-aged cadres are the backbone of our country. The operations in a hospital depend on middle-aged surgeons; the most important research projects are thrust on middle-aged scientists and technicians; the hardest jobs in industry are given to middle-aged workers; the chief courses in school are taught by middle-aged teachers . . .'

'Don't go on and on!' Jiang put in. 'Why should a doctor worry about all that?'

Liu screwed up his eyes and continued half tipsy, 'Didn't Lu You say, "Though in a humble position I remain concerned for my country?" I'm a doctor no one has ever heard of, but I keep affairs of state in mind. Everyone acknowledges the key role of the middle-aged, but who knows how hard their life is? At work they shoulder a heavy load, at home they have all the housework. They have to support their parents and bring up their children. They play a key role not just because of their experience and ability, but because they put up with hardships and make great sacrifices—as do their wives and children.'

Lu had listened blankly. Now she interposed softly, 'It's a pity so few people realize that.' Fu, who had been speechless, filled Liu's cup and declared cheerfully, 'You should have studied sociology.'

Liu laughed sarcastically. 'If I had, I'd have been a big Rightist! Sociologists have to study social evils.'

'If you uncover them and set them right, society can make progress. That's to the left not the right,' said Fu.

'Never mind, I don't want to be either. But I really am interested in social problems. For instance, the problem of the middle-aged.' Liu rested his elbows on the table, toying with his empty cup, and began again. 'There used to be a saying, "At middle age a man gives up all activities." That was true in the old society when people aged prematurely. By forty they felt they were old. But now that saying should be changed to "At middle age a man is frantically busy!" Right? this reflects the fact that in our new society people are younger, full of vitality. Middle age is a time to give full play to one's abilities.'

'Well said!' Fu approved.

'Don't be in such a hurry to express approval. I've another crazy notion.' Liu gripped Fu's arm and continued eagerly, 'Looking at it that way, you can say our middle-aged generation is lucky to be alive at this time. But in fact we're an unlucky generation.'

'You're monopolizing the conversation!' protested Jiang.

But Fu said, 'I'd like to hear why we're unlucky.'

'Unlucky because the time when we could have done our

best work was disrupted by Lin Biao and the "gang of four",'
Liu sighed. 'Take your case, you nearly became an unemployed
vagrant. Now we middle-aged people are the ones chiefly
responsible for modernization, and we don't feel up to it. We
haven't the knowledge, energy or strength. We're
overburdened—that's our tragedy.'

'There's no pleasing you!' laughed Jiang. 'When you're not
used, you complain that your talents are wasted, you live at the
wrong time. When you're fully used, you gripe that you're
overworked and underpaid!'

'Don't you ever complain?' her husband retorted.

Jiang hung her head and did not answer.

All Liu had said had given Lu the impression that he felt
impelled to leave not entirely for his daughter's sake, but also
for his own.

Once more Liu raised his cup and cried, 'Come on! Let's
drink to middle age!'

10

After their guests had gone and the children were asleep, Lu
washed up in the kitchen. In their room, she found her
husband, leaning against the bed, deep in thought, his hand on
his forehead.

'A penny for them, Jiajie.' Lu was surprised he looked so
depressed.

Fu asked in reply, 'Do you remember Petöfi's poem?'

'Of course!'

'I wish I were a crumbling ruin . . .' Fu removed his hand
from his forehead. 'I'm a ruin now, like an old man. Going bald
and grey. I can feel the lines on my forehead. I'm a ruin!'

He did look older than his age. Upset, Lu touched his
forehead. 'It's my fault! We're such a burden to you!'

Fu took her hand and held it lovingly. 'No. You're not to
blame.'

'I'm a selfish woman, who thinks only about her work.' Lu's
voice quivered. She couldn't take her eyes away from his
forehead. 'I have a home but I've paid it little attention. Even

when I'm not working, my mind is preoccupied with my patients. I haven't been a good wife or mother.'

'Don't be silly! I know more than anyone how much you've sacrificed!' He stopped as tears welled up in his eyes.

Nestling up against him, she said sadly, 'You've aged. I don't want you to grow old . . .'

'Never mind. "If my love green ivy would be, she'd tenderly entwine around my lonely head."' Softly he recited their favourite poem.

In the still autumn night, Lu fell asleep against her husband's chest, her lashes moist with tears. Fu put her carefully on the bed. Opening her eyes she asked, 'Did I fall asleep?'

'You're very tired.'

'No. I'm not.'

Fu propped himself up and said to her, 'Even metal has fatigue. A microscopic crack is formed first, and it develops until a fracture suddenly occurs.'

That was Fu's field of research, and he often mentioned it. But this time, his words carried weight and left a deep impression on Lu.

A dreadful fatigue, a dreadful fracture. In the quiet of the night, Lu seemed to hear the sound of breaking. The props of heavy bridges, sleepers under railways, old bricks and the ivy creeping up ruins . . . all these were breaking.

11

The night deepened.

The pendent lamp in the room having been turned off, the wall lamp shed a dim blue light.

Before her eyes flitted two blue dots of light, like fireflies on a summer night or a will-o'-the-wisp in the wilderness, which turned into Qin's cold stare when she looked carefully.

Qin, however, had been warm and kind when she summoned Lu to Jiao's room the morning he entered the hospital. 'Sit down please, Dr Lu. Old Jiao has gone to have his ECG done. He'll be back in a minute.'

All smiles, she had risen from an armchair in a room in a

quiet building with red-carpeted corridors reserved for high cadres.

Qin had asked her to sit in the other armchair, while she went over to the locker beside the bed and got out a basket of tangerines, which she placed on the side table between the chairs.

'Have a tangerine.'

Lu declined. 'No, thank you.'

'Try one. They were sent to me by a friend in the south. They're very good.' She took one and offered it to her.

Lu took it, but held it in her hand. Qin's new friendliness sent a chill down her spine. She was still conscious of the coldness in Qin's eyes when they had first met.

'What actually is a cataract, Dr Lu? Some doctors told me that an operation is not suitable for all cases.' Qin's manner was humble and ingratiating.

'A growth which progressively covers the eyeball, destroying the sight.' Looking at the tangerine in her hand, Lu explained, 'It can be divided into stages. It's better to have the operation done when the cataract is mature.'

'I see. What happens if it isn't done then?'

'The lens shrinks as the cortex is absorbed. The suspensory ligament becomes fragile. The difficulty of the operation increases as the lens is liable to be dislocated.'

Qin nodded.

She had not understood nor tried to understand what she had been told. Lu wondered why she had bothered to ask questions. Just passing time? Having started her ward duty only that morning, she had to familiarize herself with the cases of her patients and attend to them. She couldn't sit there, making small talk. She wanted to check Jiao's eyes if he returned soon.

Qin had more questions for her. 'I heard there was an artificial lens abroad. The patient needn't wear a convex lens after an operation. Is that right?'

Lu nodded. 'We're experimenting on that too.'

Qin inquired eagerly, 'Can you put one in for my husband?'

Lu smiled. 'I said it's still at the experimental stage. I don't think he'd want one now, do you?'

'No.' Of course she didn't want him to be a guinea-pig. 'What is the procedure for his operation?'

Lu was baffled. 'What do you mean?'

'Shouldn't you map out a plan in case something unexpected crops up?' As Lu looked blank, she added, 'I've often read about it in the papers. Sometimes surgeons form a team to discuss and work out a plan.'

Lu couldn't help laughing. 'No need for that! This is a very simple operation.'

Disgruntled, Qin looked away. Then she turned back and pressed her point patiently with a smile, 'Underestimating the enemy often leads to failure. This has happened in the history of our Party.' Then she got Lu to describe certain situations which could cause the operation to fail.

'One has to think twice about patients with heart trouble, hypertension or bronchitis. Coughing can create problems.'

'That's just what I feared,' Qin cried, striking the arm of her chair. 'My husband's heart isn't good and he has high blood pressure.'

'We always examine the patient thoroughly before an operation,' Lu consoled her.

'He has bronchitis too.'

'Has he been coughing lately?'

'No. But what if he does on the operating-table? What shall we do?'

Why was she so anxious, Lu wondered, looking at her watch. The morning was almost gone. Her glance fell on the white lace curtain hanging beside the French windows and tension gripped her when the footsteps approaching the door moved away again. After a long time, Jiao, a blue and white dressing-gown round his shoulders, was helped in by a nurse.

Qin commented, 'It's taken you a long time!'

Jiao shook Lu's hand and flopped down exhausted in the armchair. 'There were lots of examinations. I had a blood test, an X-ray, and an ECG. The staff were all very kind to me. I didn't have to wait my turn.'

He sipped the cup of tea Qin handed him. 'I never thought an eye operation involved so many tests.'

Lu read the reports. 'The X-ray and the ECG are normal. Your blood pressure's a bit high.'

Qin piped up. 'How high?'

'150 over 100. But that doesn't matter.' Then she asked, 'Have you been coughing recently, Vice-minister Jiao?'

'No,' he answered lightly.

Qin pressed, 'Can you guarantee that you won't cough on the operating-table?'

'Well . . .' Jiao was not so sure.

'That's important, Old Jiao,' Qin warned him gravely. 'Dr Lu just told me that if you cough, the eyeball can fall out.'

Jiao turned to Lu. 'How can I be certain I won't cough?'

'It's not that serious. If you are a smoker, don't smoke before the operation.'

'OK.'

Qin pressed again. 'But what if you should cough? What will happen?'

Lu laughed. 'Don't worry, Comrade Qin. We can sew up the incision and open it again after he stops coughing.'

'That's right,' said Jiao. 'When I had my right eye operated on, it was sewn up and then opened again. But it wasn't because I coughed!'

Curiosity made Lu ask, 'Why then?'

Jiao put down his cup and took out his cigarette case, but put it away again remembering Lu's advice. With a sigh he related, 'I'd been labelled as a traitor and was having a difficult time. When the sight went in my right eye I had an operation. Soon after it started, the rebels came and tried to force the surgeon not to treat me. I nearly choked with indignation, but the doctor calmly sewed up the incision, threw the rebels out and then removed the cataract.'

'Really?' Stunned, Lu asked, 'Which hospital was that?'

'This one.'

A coincidence? She looked at Jiao again to see whether she had seen him before, but could not recognize him.

Ten years ago, she had been operating on a so-called traitor when she had been interrupted by some rebels. That patient's name was Jiao. So it *was* he! Later, the rebels from Jiao's department, collaborating with a rebel in the hospital, put up a slogan claiming that 'Lu Wenting betrays the proletariat by operating on the traitor Jiao Chengsi.'

No wonder she hadn't recognized him. Ten years ago, Jiao, sallow and depressed, dressed in an old cotton-padded coat, had come to the hospital alone as an ordinary patient. Lu suggested an operation and made an appointment, which he kept. When she began operating she heard the nurse saying outside, 'No admittance. This is the operating theatre.'

Then she heard shouting and noises. 'Shit! He's a traitor. We're against treating traitors.'

'We won't allow stinking intellectuals to treat traitors.'

'Force open the door!'

Jiao, indignant, said on the operating-table, 'Let me go blind, doctor. Don't do it.'

Lu warned him against moving and quickly sewed up the incision.

Three men charged in, while the more timid ones hesitated at the door. Lu sat there immobile.

Jiao said the doctor had thrown them out. As a matter of fact, Lu had not. She had sat on the stool by the operating-table in her white gown, green plastic slippers, blue cap and mask. All that could be seen of her were her eyes and her bare arms above the rubber gloves. The rebels were awed perhaps by her strange appearance, the solemn atmosphere of the operating theatre and the bloody eye exposed through a hole in the white towel covering the patient. Lu said tersely from behind her mask, 'Get out, please!'

The rebels looked at each other and left.

When Lu resumed work, Jiao told her, 'Don't do it, doctor, they'll only blind me again even if you cure me. And you may get involved.'

'Keep quiet.' Lu worked swiftly. When she was bandaging him, all she had said was, 'I'm a doctor.' That was how it had happened.

The rebels from Jiao's department, coming to the hospital to put up a big-character poster denouncing her for curing a traitor, had created quite a sensation. But what did it matter? She was already being criticized for being a bourgeois specialist. These charges and this operation had not left much impression on her. She had forgotten all about it, until Jiao had brought it up.

'I really respect her, Dr Lu. She was a true doctor,' Qin sighed. 'Pity the hospital kept no records then. I can't find out who she was. Yesterday I expressed my wish to Director Zhao to have her operate on my husband.' Lu's awkward expression made her add, 'I'm sorry, Dr Lu. Since Director Zhao has confidence in you, we will too. I hope you won't let him down. Learn from that doctor. Of course, we've a lot to learn from her too, don't you agree?'

Lu had no alternative but to nod.

'You're still young,' Qin said encouragingly. 'I heard you haven't joined the Party yet. You must strive for it, Comrade.'

Lu told her frankly, 'I don't have a good class background.'

'That's not the way to look at things. You can't choose your family but you can choose what you do with your life.' Qin was eloquent and enthusiastic. 'Our Party does pay attention to class origins, but not exclusively. It's your attitude that counts. When you draw the line between yourself and your family, get close to the Party and make contributions to the people, then the Party will open its doors to you.'

Lu crossed the room to draw the curtain and examined Jiao's eye. Then she told Jiao, 'If it's all right with you. let's do the operation the day after tomorrow.'

Jiao answered briskly, 'All right. The earlier the better.'

It was already after six when Lu took her leave. Qin hurried out after her. 'Are you going home, Dr Lu?'

'Yes.'

'Shall I arrange for Jiao's car to take you?'

'No, thank you.' Lu declined with a wave of her hand.

12

It was almost midnight, the ward was very quiet. A single wall lamp cast a pale blue light on an intravenous drip, from which the medicine was dropping, as if the only sign of Dr Lu's life.

Fu, sitting at the side of the bed, stared blankly at his wife. It was the first time that he had sat alone with her since her collapse, probably the first time that he had looked at her so intently for the past dozen years.

He remembered that once he had fixed his eyes on her for a long time, and she had asked, her head on one side, 'Why do you look at me like that?' Sheepishly he had turned his eyes away. That was when they were courting. But now she could neither move her head nor speak. Vulnerable, she was unable to raise a protest.

Only then did he notice that she looked surprisingly frail and old! Her jet-black hair was streaked with grey; her firm, tender skin, loose and soft; and there were lines on her forehead. The corners of her mouth, once so pretty, were now drooping. Her life, like a dying flame, was petering out fast. He could not believe that his wife, a firm character, had become so feeble overnight!

She was not weak, he knew that well. Slim in build, she was in fact fit and strong. Though her shoulders were slight, she silently endured all hardships and sudden misfortunes. She never complained, feared or became disheartened.

'You're a tough woman,' he had often said to her.

'Me? No, I'm timid. Not tough at all.' Her answer was always the same.

Only the night before she had fallen ill, she had made, as Fu put it, another 'heroic decision' that he should move to his institute.

Xiaojia had quite recovered by then. After Yuanyuan had done his homework, the children went to bed. At last there was peace in the small room.

Autumn had come, the wind was cold. The kindergarten had asked parents for their children's winter clothes. Lu took out the cotton-padded coat Xiaojia had worn the previous year, ripped it apart, made it bigger and sewed on a new pair of cuffs. Then she spread it out on the desk and added a layer of new cotton padding.

Fu took his unfinished article from the bookcase and,

hesitating for a brief second beside the desk, sat down on the bed.

'Just a moment,' Lu said without turning her head, hurrying, 'I'll soon finish.'

When she removed the coat from the desk, Fu remarked, 'If only we could have another small room. Even six square metres, just big enough for a desk.'

Lu listened, lowering her head, busy sewing. After a while, she hastily folded up the unfinished coat and said, 'I've got to go to the hospital now. You can have the desk.'

'But why? It's late,' he queried.

She said, while putting on her jacket, 'There will be two operations tomorrow morning and I want to check how the patients are. I'll go and have a look at them.'

She often went to the hospital in the evening in fact. So Fu teased her, saying, 'Though you're here at home, your heart's still in the hospital.'

'Put on more clothes. It's cold,' he urged.

'I won't be long,' she said quickly. With an apologetic smile, she continued, 'Two funny patients, you know. One's a vice-minister. His wife's been worrying to death about the operation and making an awful fuss. So I must go to see him. The other's a little girl. She told me today that she had a lot of nightmares and slept badly.'

'OK, doc!' He smiled. 'Get going and come back soon!'

She left. When she returned he was still burning the midnight oil. Not wanting to disturb him, she said after tucking in the children. 'I'm going to bed first.'

He looked round, saw she was in bed and again buried himself in his papers and books. But soon he sensed that she had not fallen asleep. Was it perhaps the light? He bent the lamp lower, shielded the light with a newspaper and carried on with his work.

After a while, he heard her soft, even snoring. But he knew that she was faking. Many times, she had tried to pretend she was sound asleep, so he could feel at ease studying late. In fact he had long since seen through her little trick, but had no heart to expose it.

Some time later, he got to his feet, stretched and said, 'All right! I'll sleep too.'

'Don't worry about me!' Lu said quickly. 'I'm already half asleep.'

Standing with his hands on the edge of the desk, he hesitated, looking at his unfinished article. Then he made up his mind and said, closing all the books, 'I'll call it a day.'

'How about your article? How can you finish it if you don't make full use of your nights?'

'One night can't make up for ten years.'

Lu sat up, threw a sweater over her shoulders and said in earnest, her head against the bed board, 'Guess what I've been thinking just now?'

'You oughtn't to have thought of anything! Now close *your* eyes. You'll have to cure other people's eyes tomorrow.'

'It's no joke. Listen, I think you should move into your institute. Then you'll have more time.'

Fu stared at her. Her face was glowing, her eyes dancing. Obviously she was very pleased with the idea.

She went on, 'I'm serious. You've things to do. I know, the children and I have been hampering you.'

'Come off it! It's not you . . .'

Lu broke in, 'Of course it is! We can't divorce. The children need their father, and a scientist needs his family. However, we must think of some way to turn your eight working hours into sixteen.'

'But the children and the housework will all fall on you. That won't do!'

'Why not? Even without you, we can manage.'

He listed all the problems, to which she answered one by one. Finally she said, 'Haven't you often remarked that I'm a tough woman? I can cope. Your son won't go hungry, your daughter won't be ill-treated.'

He was convinced. So they decided to have a try the next day.

'It's so very difficult to do something in China!' Fu said undressing. 'During the war, many old revolutionaries died for a new China. Now to modernize our country, again our generation has to make sacrifices through hardly anyone notices it.'

He kept talking to himself like this. When he put his clothes on the back of a chair and turned to get into bed, he saw that Lu had fallen asleep. With a faint smile on her face, she looked pleased with her proposal, even in her dreams.

But who would imagine their trial would fail on the very first day?

13

The operations were successful, though Lu's private plan failed.

That morning when she had entered the ward ten minutes early as usual, Dr Sun was already there waiting for her.

'Good morning, Dr Lu,' he greeted her, 'we've got a donor's eye today. Can we fit in the corneal transplant?'

'Excellent! We've got a patient who's anxious to have the operation done as soon as possible,' Lu exclaimed in delight.

'But you already have two operations scheduled for this morning. Do you think you can manage a third?'

'Sure,' she replied, straightening up as if showing him that she was perfectly capable.

'OK, it's settled then.' He had made up his mind.

Holding the arm of Jiang, who had just arrived, Lu headed for the operating theatre. She was in high spirits, walking with a spring in her step, as though on an outing.

The operating theatres of this hospital, occupying a whole floor, were large and impressive. The big characters 'Operating Theatre' in red paint on the beige glass door were striking. When a wheeled stretcher bearing a patient was pushed through this door, his relatives remained outside, anxiously looking at the mysterious, perhaps even frightening place, as if Death were lurking about inside.

But in fact, the operating theatre was a place of hope. Inside, the walls along the wide corridor were painted a light, agreeable green. Here there were the operating theatres for the various departments. The surgeons, their assistants, anaesthetists and theatre nurses scurried to and fro lightly. No laughter, no chatter. This was the most quiet, most orderly area of the large hospital, into which more than a thousand patients poured every day.

Vice-minister Jiao was brought into one of these theatres, and then put on a high cream-coloured operating-table. His head was covered by a sterilized white towel. There was an olive-shaped hole in it revealing one of the eyes.

Lu already in her overall sat on a stool near the operating-table, her gloved hands raised. The height of the stool was adjustable. Lu, being small, had to raise it whenever she operated. But today, it had already been adjusted. She turned and glanced at Jiang gratefully, realising she had done it.

A nurse pushed the surgical instrument table nearer to Lu. The adjustable plate was now placed above the patient's chest, within the surgeon's reach.

'Shall we start now?' Lu asked watching Jiao's eye. 'Try to relax. We'll first inject the local anaesthetic. Then your eye will feel numb. The operation won't take long.'

At this, Jiao suddenly cried out, 'Steady on!'

What was wrong? Both Lu and Jiang were taken aback. Jiao pulled away the towel from his face, striving to raise his head. He inquired, pointing at Lu, 'It was you, Dr Lu, who operated before on my eye?'

Lu quickly raised her gloved hands lest he touch them. Before she could speak, he went on emotionally, 'Yes, it was you. It must have been you! You said the same words. Even your tone and intonation are the same!'

'Yes, it was me,' Lu had to admit.

'Why didn't you tell me before? I'm so grateful to you.'

'Never mind . . .' Lu could not find anything else to say. She cast a glance at the towel, beckoned the nurse to change it. Then she said again, 'Shall we start, Vice-minister Jiao?'

Jiao sighed. It was hard for him to calm down. Lu had to say in a commanding tone, 'Don't move. Don't speak. We'll start now.'

She skilfully injected some novocaine into his lower eyelid and began the operation. She had performed such operations umpteen times, but every time she picked up her instruments, she felt like a raw recruit on the battlefield. Lu held out two tapering fingers to pick up a needle-holder which looked like a small pair of scissors. She fixed the needle to the instrument.

'What's the matter?' Jiang asked softly.

Instead of answering, Lu held the hook-shaped needle up to the light to examine it.

'Is this a new one?'

Jiang had no idea, so they both turned to the nurse.

'A new needle?'

The nurse stepped forward and said in a low voice, 'Yes, a new one.'

Lu had another look at the needle pin and grumbled, 'How can we use such a needle?'

Lu and some other doctors had complained many times about the poor quality of their surgical instruments. However, faulty ones appeared from time to time. Lu could do nothing about it. When she found good scalpels, scissors and needles, she would ask the nurse to keep them for her for later use.

She had no idea that all the surgical instruments had been replaced by new ones that day, but unfortunately there was a bad needle among them. Whenever such things occurred, Lu's good-natured face would change, and she would reprimand the nurse. The young nurse, though innocent perhaps, could not defend herself. There was nothing to say in the circumstances. A blunt needle not only prolonged the operation, but also increased the patient's suffering.

Frowning, Lu said quietly, so that Jiao could not overhear, 'Bring me another!

It was an order, and the nurse picked out an old needle from a sterilizer.

The theatre nurses respected Lu, while at the same time being afraid of her. They admired her skill and feared her strictness. A doctor's authority was established through his scalpel. A good oculist could give a blind man back his sight, while a bad one might blind him permanently. Lu had no position, no power, but through her scalpel she wielded authority.

The operation was almost complete, when Jiao's body jerked suddenly.

'Don't move!' Lu warned him.

'Don't move!' Jiang repeated quickly. 'What's the matter?'

'I . . . want to . . . cough!' a strangled voice sounded from under the towel.

This was just what his wife had feared would happen. Why choose this moment to cough? Was it psychological? A conditioned reflex?

'Can you control it for a minute?'

'No, I . . . I can't.' His chest was heaving.

There was no time to lose! Lu hurriedly took emergency measures, while calming him down, 'Just a second! Breathe out and hold your cough!'

She was quickly tying up the suture while he exhaled, his chest moving vigorously as if he would die of suffocation at any moment. When the last knot was done, Lu sighed with relief and said, 'You can cough now, but not too loudly.'

But he did not. On the contrary, his breath gradually grew even and normal.

'Go ahead and cough. It won't matter,' Jiang urged again.

'I'm awfully sorry,' Jiao apologized. 'I'm all right now. Carry on with the operation please.'

Jiang rolled her eyes, wanting to give him a piece of her mind. A man of his age should know better. Lu threw her a glance, and Jiang bit back her resentment. They smiled knowingly at each other. It was all in the day's work!

Lu snipped off the knots and started the operation again. It continued without a hitch. Afterwards Lu got off the stool and sat at a small table to write out a prescription, while Jiao was moved back on to the wheeled stretcher. As it was being pushed out, Jiao suddenly called to Lu, like a kid who has misbehaved, his voice trembling slightly.

Lu stepped over to him. His eyes had been bandaged. 'Anything I can do?' she stooped to ask.

He reached out, groping. When he caught hold of her hands, still in their gloves, he shook them vigorously. 'I've given you much trouble on both occasions. I'm so sorry . . .'

Lu was stunned for a brief moment. Then she consoled him, looking at his bandaged face, 'Never mind. Have a good rest. We'll take off the bandage in a few days.'

After he was wheeled out, Lu glanced at the clock. A forty-minute operation had lasted an hour. She took off her white gown and rubber gloves and immediately donned another. As Lu turned to let the nurse tie the gown at the back, Jiang asked, 'Shall we continue?'

'Yes.'

14

'Let me do the next operation,' Jiang begged. 'You take a short rest, then do the third.'

Lu shook her head and said smilingly, 'I'll do it. You're not familiar with Wang Xiaoman. The child's scared stiff. We became friends during the last few days. Better leave her to me.'

The girl did not come into the operating theatre on a wheeled stretcher, but was almost dragged in. In a white gown, which was a bit too large for her, she was reluctant to go anywhere near the operating-table.

'Aunt Lu, I'm scared. I don't want the operation. Please go and explain to my mother.'

The sight of the doctors and nurses in such strange clothes terrified her. Her heart was pounding, as she tried to wrench away from the nurses, pleading with Lu for help.

Lu walked towards the table and coaxed her with a grin, 'Come on, little girl. Didn't you promise to have this operation? Be brave! There's nothing to fear. You won't feel any pain once you've been given some anaesthetic.'

Xiaoman sized up Lu in her funny clothes and gazed at her kind, smiling, encouraging eyes. Then she climbed up on to the operating-table. A nurse spread a towel over her face. Lu motioned the nurse to tie up her hands. As the little patient was about to protest, Lu said, perching on the table, 'Xiaoman, be a good girl! It's the same for all patients. Really, it won't take long.' She gave her an injection of the anaesthetic while telling her, 'I'm giving you an injection and soon your eye will feel nothing at all.'

Lu was both doctor, devoted mother and kindergarten nurse. She took the scissors, forceps and other instruments which Jiang handed to her while keeping up a running commentary for the benefit of the girl. When she severed the straight muscle which caused the squint, Xiaoman's nerve was affected and she became nauseous.

'You feel a little sick?' Lu asked. 'Take a deep breath. Just hold on for a minute. That's better. Still sick? Feeling any better? We'll finish the operation very soon. There's a good girl!'

Lu's words lulled Xiaoman into a trance, while the operation continued. When she had been bandaged and wheeled out of the room, she remembered what her mother had told her to say, so she called out sweetly, 'Thank you very much, aunty.'

Everyone burst out laughing. The minute hand of the clock on the wall had just moved half an hour.

Lu was wet with sweat, the perspiration beading on her forehead, her underwear soaking. Wet patches showed under her armpits. She was surprised at this because it was not hot. Why had she perspired so profusely? She slightly moved her numb arms, which had ached from being raised for the duration of the operation.

When she removed the operating gown again and reached out for another, she suddenly felt dizzy. She closed her eyes for a minute, shook her head several times and then slowly eased one of her arms into a sleeve. A nurse came to help her tie the gown.

'Dr Lu!' the nurse exclaimed suddenly. 'Your lips are so pale!'

Jiang, who was also changing, turned to look at Lu. 'Goodness!' she said in astonishment. 'You do look very pale!'

It was true. There were black rings under her eyes, even her lids were puffy. She looked a patient herself!

Seeing that Jiang's startled eyes remained fixed on her, Lu grinned and said, 'Stop fussing! It'll soon be over.'

She had no doubt that she could carry on with the next

operation. Had she not worked like this for years?

'Shall we continue?' the nurse queried.

'Yes, of course.'

How could they afford to stop? The donor's eye could not be stored too long, nor the operation be delayed. They had to go on working.

'Wenting,' Jiang stepped over to Lu and suggested, 'Let's have a break for half an hour.'

Lu looked at the clock. It was just after ten. If they postponed it for half an hour, some colleagues would be late for lunch, while others had to rush home to prepare a meal for their children.

'Continue?' the nurse asked again.

'Yes.'

15

Doctors of this and other hospitals who were undergoing further training thronged the door talking to Lu. They had got special permission to see her operate.

Uncle Zhang, helped by a nurse, clambered on to the operating-table, still talking and laughing.

The table was a bit too small for him and his feet and hands dangled over the side. He had a loud voice and talked incessantly, joking with a nurse, 'Don't laugh at me, girl. If the medical team hadn't come to our village and persuaded me to have this operation, I'd rather die than let you cut my eye with a knife. Just imagine! A steel knife cutting into my flesh, ugh! Who knows if it will do me some good or not? Ha! Ha! . .'

The young nurse tittered and said softly, 'Uncle, lower your voice please.'

'I know, young lady. We must keep quiet in a hospital, mustn't we?' he still boomed. Gesticulating busily with one hand, he went on, 'You can't imagine how I felt when I heard that my eye could be cured. I wanted to laugh and, at the same time, to cry. My father went blind in his old age and died a blind man. I never dreamed that a blind man like me could see the sun again. Times have really changed, haven't they?'

The nurse giggled while covering him with a towel. 'Don't move again, uncle?' she said. 'This towel's been sterilized, don't touch it.'

'All right,' he answered gravely. 'Since I'm in hospital, I should obey the rules.' But he was trying to raise his strong arms again.

Worrying about his restlessness, the nurse said, holding a strap, 'I'll have to tie your arms to the table, uncle. That's the rule here.'

Zhang was puzzled, but soon chortled. 'Truss me up, eh?' he joked. 'OK, go ahead! To be frank, lass, if it were not for my eyes, I wouldn't be so obedient. Though blind, I go to the fields twice a day. I was born a lively character. I like to be on the go. I just can't sit still.'

This made the nurse laugh, and he himself chuckled too. But he stopped immediately when Lu entered. He asked, cocking up his ears. 'Is that you, Dr Lu? I can recognize your steps. It's funny, since I lost my sight, my ears have grown sharp.'

Seeing him full of beans, Lu could not help laughing. She took her seat, preparing for the operation. When she picked up the precious donor's cornea from a phial and sewed it on to a piece of gauze, he piped up again, 'So an eye can be replaced? I never knew that!'

'It's not replacing the whole eye, just a filmy membrane,' Jiang corrected him.

'Can't see the difference.' He wasn't interested in details. With a sigh, he continued, 'It needs much skill, doesn't it? When I return to my village with a pair of good eyes, the villagers'll say I must have met some kind fairy. Ha! Ha! I'll tell them I met Dr Lu!'

Jiang tittered, winking at Lu, who felt a little embarrassed. Still sewing, she explained, 'Other doctors can do the same.'

'That's quite true,' he agreed. ''You only find good doctors in this big hospital. No kidding!'

Her preparations over, Lu parted his eyelids with a speculum and said, 'We'll start now. Just relax.'

Zhang was not like other patients, who only listened to whatever the doctors said. He thought it impolite not to answer. So he said understandingly, 'I'm perfectly all right. Go ahead. I don't mind if it's painful. Of course, it hurts to cut with a scalpel or a pair of scissors. But don't worry about me. I trust you. Besides . . .'

Jiang had to stop him, still smiling. 'Uncle, don't talk any more.'

Finally he complied.

Lu picked up a trephine, small as a pen cap, and lightly cut out the opaque cornea. Cutting a similar disc of clear cornea from the donor's eye, she transferred it to Zhang's eye. Then she began the delicate task of stitching it with the needle-holder. The suture was finer than a hair.

The operation went smoothly. When she had finished, the transplanted cornea was perfectly fixed on the surface of the eye. But for some little black knots, one could never tell it was a new cornea.

'Well done!' the doctors around the operating-table quietly exclaimed in admiration.

Lu sighed with relief. Deeply touched, Jiang looked up at her friend with feeling. Silently, she put layers of gauze over Zhang's eye . . .

As he was wheeled out, Zhang seemed to awaken from a dream. He became animated again. When the wheeled stretcher was already out the door, he cried out, 'Thanks a lot, Dr Lu!'

The operations had ended. As Lu was pulling herself to her feet, she found her legs had gone to sleep. She simply could not stand up. After a little rest, she tried again and again, till she finally made it. There was a sudden pain in her side. She pressed it with her hand, not taking it seriously for it had occurred before. Engrossed in an operation, sitting on the little stool, for hours at a time, she was aware of nothing else. But as soon as this operation had ended, she felt utterly exhausted, even too tired to move.

16

At that moment, Fu was cycling home in haste. He had not

intended to return that day. Early that morning, Fu, at his wife's suggestion, had rolled up his bedding, put it on his bicycle carrier and taken it to his office to begin his new life.

By noon, however, he was wavering. Would Lu finish her operations in time? Imagining her dragging herself home to prepare lunch for the children, he suddenly felt a pang of guilt. So he jumped on his bicycle and pedalled home.

Just as he turned into their lane, he caught sight of his wife leaning against a wall, unable to move.

'Wenting! What's wrong?' he cried out, leaping off to help.

'Nothing. I'm just a bit tired.' She put an arm round his shoulder and moved slowly towards home.

Fu noticed that she was very pale and that beads of cold sweat had broken out on her forehead.

He asked uneasily, 'Shall I take you to hospital?'

She sat down on the edge of the bed, her eyes closed, and answered, 'Don't worry. I'll be all right after a short rest.'

She pointed to the bed, too weak to say anything. Fu took off her shoes and coat.

'Lie down and get some sleep. I'll wake you later.'

He went to boil some water in a saucepan. When he came back to fetch noodles, he heard her say, 'We ought to have a rest. Shall we take the children to Beihai Park next Sunday? We haven't been there for more than ten years.'

'Fine. I'm all for it!' Fu agreed, wondering why she should suddenly want to go there.

He gave her an anxious glance and went to cook the noodles. When he returned, food in hand, she had already fallen asleep. He did not disturb her. When Yuanyuan came home, the two of them sat down to eat.

Just then, Lu began groaning. Fu put down his bowl and rushed to the bed. Lu was deathly white, her face covered in sweat.

'I can't fight it,' she said in a feeble voice, gasping for breath.

Frightened, Fu took her hand asking, 'What's wrong? Have you any pain?'

With a great effort, Lu pointed to her heart.

Panicking, Fu pulled open a drawer rummaging for a painkiller. On second thoughts, he wondered if she needed a tranquillizer.

Though in great pain, she was clear-headed. She signed to him to calm down and said with all her remaining strength, 'I must go to hospital!'

Only then did Fu realize the seriousness of her illness. For more than ten years she had never seen a doctor, though she went to the hospital every day. Now she was obviously critically ill. As he hurried out, he stopped at the door and turned to say, 'I'll go and get a taxi.'

He rushed to the public telephone on the corner. He dialled quickly and waited. When someone answered, he heard a cold voice saying, 'No taxis at the moment.'

'Look, I've got a very sick person here!'

'Still, you'll have to wait half an hour.'

Fu began to plead, when the man rang off.

He tried to call Lu's hospital, but no one seemed to be in the office of the Ophthalmic Department. He asked the operator to put him through to the vehicle dispatch office.

'We can't send you a car without an official approval slip,' was the answer.

Where on earth could he track down the hospital leaders to get an approval slip?

'But this is urgent! Hello!' he shouted into the receiver. But the line had already gone dead.

He phoned the political department which, he thought, ought to help him out. After a long time, a woman picked up the receiver. She listened patiently and said politely, 'Would you please contact the administration department?'

He had to ask the operator to put him through to the administration department. Recognizing his voice, the operator demanded impatiently, 'Where exactly do you want?'

Where? He was not sure himself. In a begging voice, he said he wanted to speak to anyone in the administration department. The telephone rang and rang. Nobody answered.

Disappointed, Fu abandoned the idea of finding a car. He headed for a small workshop in the lane making cardboard boxes, hoping to borrow a tricycle and trailer. The old lady in charge, hearing of his predicament, sympathized with him, but unfortunately could do nothing, for both her tricycles were out.

What was to be done? Standing in the alley, Fu was desperate. Sit Lu on the bicycle carrier? That was impossible.

Just then, Fu saw a van coming. Without much thought, he raised his hand to stop it.

The van came to a halt, and the driver poked his head out, staring in surprise. But when he heard what was happening, he beckoned Fu to get into the van.

They went straight to Fu's home. When the driver saw Lu being dragged towards the van supported by her husband, he hurried to help her get into the cabin. Then slowly he drove her to the casualty department of the hospital.

17

She had never slept so long, never felt so tired. She felt pain all over her body as if she had just fallen from a cloud. She had not the slightest bit of strength left. After a peaceful sleep, her limbs were more relaxed, her heart calmer. But she felt her mind go blank.

For years, she had simply had no time to pause, to reflect on the hardships she had experienced or the difficulties lying ahead. Now all physical and mental burdens had been lifted. She seemed to have plenty of time to examine her past and to explore the future. But her mind had switched off; no reminiscences, no hopes. Nothing.

Perhaps it was only a dream. She had had such dreams before . . .

One evening when she was only five, a north wind had been howling. Her mother had gone out, leaving her alone at home. Soon it was very dark and her mother had not returned. For the first time, Lu felt lonely, terrified. She cried and shouted, 'Mama . . . mama . . .' This scene often appeared later in her dreams. The howling wind, the door blown open by a sudden gust and the pale kerosene lamp remained vividly in her mind. For a long time, she could not tell whether it had been true.

This time, it was not a dream but reality.

She was in bed, ill, and Jiajie was attending her. He looked flaked out too. He was dozing, half lying on the bed. He would catch cold if not awakened. She tried to call him, but no sound came out of her mouth. There was a lump in her throat choking her. She wanted to pull a coat over him, but her arms did not seem to belong to her.

She glanced round and saw she was in a single room. Only serious cases were given such special treatment. She was suddenly seized by fear. 'Am I . . .?'

The autumn wind rattled the door and windows. Darkness gathered, swallowed up the room. Lu felt clearer after a cold sweat. It was real, she knew, not a dream. This was the end of life, the beginning of death!

So this was dying; no fear, no pain, just life withering away, the senses blurring, slowly sinking, like a leaf drifting on a river.

All came to an end, inevitably. Rolling waves swept over her chest. Lu felt she was floating in the water . . .

'Mama . . . mama . . .'

She heard Xiaojia's call and saw her running along the bank. She turned back, reaching out her arms.

'Xiaojia . . . my darling daughter . . .'

But waves swept her away, and Xiaojia's face grew vague, her hoarse voice turned into sobbing.

'Mama . . . plait my hair . . .'

Why not plait her hair? The child had been in this world for six years, and her one desire was to have pigtails. Whenever she saw other girls with pigtails adorned with silk ribbons, admiration overwhelmed her little heart. But such requests were ignored. Mother had no time for that. On Monday morning, the hospital was crowded with patients and, for Lu, every minute counted.

'Mama . . . mama . . .'

She heard Yuanyuan's calling and saw the boy running after her along the bank. She turned back, stretching out her arms.

'Yuanyuan . . . Yuanyuan . . .'

A wave swept over her. When she struggled to the surface,

there was no sign of her son, only his voice in the distance.

'Mama . . . don't forget . . . my white gym shoes . . .'

A kaleidoscope of sports shoes whirled around. White and blue sneakers, sports boots, gym shoes, white shoes with red or blue bands. Buy a pair for Yuanyuan, whose shoes were already worn out. Buy a pair of white gym shoes and he would be in raptures for a month. But then the shoes disappeared and raining down were price tags: 3.1 yuan, 4.5 yuan, 6.3 yuan . . .

Now she saw Jiajie chasing after her, his running figure mirrored in the water. He was in a great hurry, his voice trembled as he called, 'Wenting, you can't leave us like this!'

How she wished that she could wait for him! He held out his hand to her, but the ruthless current raced forward and she drifted away helplessly.

'Dr Lu . . . Dr Lu . . .'

So many people were calling her, lining the banks. Yafen, Old Liu, Director Zhao, Dr Sun, all in white coats; Jiao Chengsi, Uncle Zhang and Wang Xiaoman in pyjamas. Among the other patients, she only recognized a few. They were all calling her.

I oughtn't to leave. No! There are so many things I still have to do. Xiaojia and Yuanyuan shouldn't be motherless. I mustn't bring Jiajie more sorrow. He can't afford to lose his wife so young. I can't tear myself away from the hospital, the patients. Oh no! I can't give up this miserable, yet dear life!

I won't drown! I must fight! I must remain in the world. But why am I so tired? I've no strength to resist, to struggle. I'm sinking, sinking . . .

Ah! Goodbye, Yuanyuan! Goodbye, Xiaojia! Will you miss your mother? In this last moment of my life, I love you more than ever. Oh, how I love you! Let me embrace you. Listen, my darlings, forgive your mummy who did not give you the love you deserved. Forgive your mummy who, time and time again, refrained from hugging you, pushing away your smiling faces. Forgive your mummy for leaving you while you're still so small.

Goodbye, Jiajie! You gave up everything for me! Without you, I couldn't have achieved anything. Without you, life had no meaning. Ah, you sacrificed so much for me! If I could, I would kneel down before you begging your pardon since I can never repay all your kindness and concern. Forgive me for neglecting you. I often thought I should do something more for you. I wanted to end my work regularly and prepare supper for you. I wanted to let you have the desk, hoping you would finish your article. But it's too late! How sad! I've no time now.

Goodbye, my patients! For the past eighteen years, my life was devoted to you. Whether I walked, sat or lay down, I thought only of you and your eyes! You don't know the joy I felt after curing an eye. What a pity I shall no longer feel that . . .

18

'Arrhythmia!' the doctor monitoring the screen claimed.

'Wenting! Wenting!' Fu cried out, fixing his eyes on his wife, who was struggling for breath.

The doctors and nurses on duty rushed into the room.

'Intravenous injection of lidocaine!' the doctor snapped an order.

A nurse quickly injected it, but before it was finished. Lu's lips went blue, her hands clenched, her eyes rolled upwards.

Her heart stopped beating.

The doctors began massage resuscitation. A respirator was applied to her head, which made a rhythmic sound. Then a defibrillator went into operation. When her chest was struck by this, her heart began to beat again.

'Get the ice cap ready!' the doctor in charge ordered, the sweat on his forehead.

An ice cap was put on Lu's head.

19

The pale dawn could be seen outside the window. Day had broken at last. Lu had lived through a crucial night. She now entered a new day.

A day nurse came into the room and opened the windows, letting in fresh air and the birds' merry singing. At once the pungent smell of medicine and death were dispelled. Dawn brought new hope to a frail life.

Another nurse came to take Lu's temperature, while a medical orderly brought in breakfast. Then the doctor on duty dropped in on his ward round.

Wang Xiaoman, still bandaged, pleaded with a nurse, 'Let me have a look at Dr Lu! Just one peep.'

'No. She nearly died last night. No one's allowed to see her for the time being.'

'Aunt, perhaps you don't know, but she fell ill because she operated on me. Please let me go and see her. I promise not to say a word to her.'

'No, no, no!' The nurse scowled.

'Oh please! Just one glance.' Xiaoman was close to tears. Hearing footsteps behind her, she turned and saw Old Zhang coming, led by his grandson.

'Grandpa,' she rushed to him, 'will you have a word with this aunt? She won't let me . . .'

Zhang, with his eyes bandaged, was dragged over by the little girl to the nurse.

'Sister, do let us have a look at her.'

Now with this old man pestering her too, the nurse flared up, 'What's the matter with you people, fooling about in the wards?'

'Come off it! Don't you understand?' Zhang's voice was not so loud today. He went on humbly, 'We've a good reason, you know. Why is Dr Lu ill? Because she operated on us. To be frank, I can't really see her, but to stand beside her bed for a while will calm my nerves.'

He was so sincere that the nurse softened and explained patiently, 'It's not that I'm being mean. Dr Lu's seriously ill with heart trouble. She mustn't be excited. You want her to recover very soon, don't you? Better not disturb her at the moment.'

'Yes, you're quite right.' Zhang sighed and sat down on a bench. Slapping his thigh, he said regretfully, 'It's all my fault. I urged her to do the operation as quickly as possible. But who would've thought . . ? What shall I do if anything happens to her?' He lowered his head in remorse.

Dr Sun hurried to see Lu too before starting his work, but was stopped by Xiaoman.

'Dr Sun, are you going to see Dr Lu?' she asked.

He nodded.

'Will you take me along? Please.'

'Not now. Some time later. OK?'

Hearing Sun's voice, Zhang stood up and reached out for him. Tugging Sun's sleeve, he said, 'Dr Sun. We'll do as you say. But can I have a word with you? I know you're extremely busy. But I still want you to listen to what's been bothering me.'

Sun patted Zhang on the shoulder and said, 'Go ahead.'

'Dr Lu's a very good doctor. Your leaders ought to do your best to cure her. If you save her, she can save many others. There are good medicines, aren't there? Give her them. Don't hesitate. I hear you have to pay for certain precious medicines. Lu's got two children. She's not well off. Now she's ill. I don't expect she can afford them. Can't this big hospital subsidize her?'

He stopped, holding Sun's hands, slightly cocking his ear towards him, waiting for his answer.

Sun had a one-track mind. He never showed his feelings. But today he was moved. Shaking Zhang's hands, he said emotionally, 'We'll do everything possible to save her!'

Zhang seemed satisfied. He called his grandson to come nearer, and groped for a satchel which was slung across the boy's shoulder.

'Here are some eggs. Please take them to her when you go in.'

'It's not necessary,' Sun replied quickly.

This put Zhang's back up instantly. Gripping Sun's hands, he raised his voice, 'If you don't take them to her, I won't let you go!'

Sun had to accept the satchel of eggs. He decided to ask a nurse to return it and explain later. As though guessing what was in Sun's mind, Zhang continued, 'And don't ask someone to bring them back.'

Forced to acquiesce, Sun helped Zhang and Xiaoman down

the stairs.

Qin, accompanied by Director Zhao, approached Lu's room. 'Zhao,' the woman talked while walking, rather excitedly, 'I was like a bureaucrat. I didn't know it was Dr Lu who had operated on Old Jiao. But you should have known, shouldn't you? Luckily Jiao recognized Lu. Otherwise we'd still be in the dark.'

'I was sent to work in the countryside at that time,' Zhao replied helplessly.

Shortly after they had entered the room, Sun arrived. The doctor on duty gave a brief report of the emergency measures taken to save Lu the previous night. Zhao looked over the case-history, nodding. Then he said, 'We must watch her carefully.'

Fu, seeing so many people entering, had stood up. But Qin, unaware of his presence, quickly sat down on the vacant stool.

'Feeling better, Dr Lu?' she asked.

Lu's eyes opened slightly but she said nothing.

'Vice-minister Jiao has told me all about you,' Qin said warmly. 'He's very grateful to you. He would have come himself if I hadn't stopped him. I'm here to thank you on his behalf. Anything you fancy eating, anything you want, let me know. I can help you. Don't stand on ceremony. We're all revolutionary comrades.'

Lu closed her eyes.

'You're still young. Be optimistic. Since you're sick, it's better to accept it. This . . .'

Zhao stopped her by saying, 'Comrade Qin Bo, let her have some rest. She's only just regained consciousness.'

'Fine, fine. Have a good rest,' Qin said, rising to her feet. 'I'll come again in a couple of days.'

Out of the ward, Qin complained frowning, 'Director Zhao, I must give you a piece of my mind. Dr Lu's a real treasure. If you had been more concerned about her, she wouldn't have become so ill. The middle-aged comrades are the backbone of our country. It's imperative to value talented people.'

'Right,' was Zhao's reply.

Gazing after her receding figure, Fu asked Sun in a small voice, 'Who's she?'

Sun looked over the frame of his spectacles at the doorway and answered frowning, 'An old lady spouting revolutionary phrases!'

20

That day, Lu was slightly better and could open her eyes easily. She drank two spoonfuls of milk and a sip of orange juice. But she lay with her eyes blank, staring at the ceiling. She wore a vacant expression, as if indifferent to everything, including her own critical condition and the unhappiness of her family. She seemed weary of life.

Fu stared at her in mute horror for he had never seen her like this before. He called her again and again, but she only responded with a slight wave of her hand, as though not wishing to be disturbed. Probably she felt comfortable letting her mind remain suspended.

Time passed unheeded. Fu, sitting at her bedside, had not slept for two nights. He felt exhausted. Dozing, he was suddenly awoken by a heart-rending scream, which shook the whole ward. He heard a girl wailing next door, 'Mama! Mama!' and a man's sobbing. Then there came the sound of footsteps as many people rushed to the room. Fu hurried out too. He saw a wheeled stretcher being pushed out of the room, on which lay a corpse covered with a sheet. Then the nurse in white pushing the stretcher appeared. A girl of sixteen with dishevelled hair stumbled out, shaking, and threw herself at the stretcher. Clutching at it with trembling hands, she pleaded, tears streaming down her cheeks, 'Don't take it away! Please! My mother's asleep. She'll soon wake up! I know she will!'

Visitors made way for the wheeled stretcher. In silence, they paid their respects to the deceased.

Fu stood rooted amid the crowd. His cheekbones stuck out prominently in his haggard face. His bloodshot eyes began to fill with tears. Clenching his fists, he tried to pull himself together, but shook all over. Unnerved by the girl's shrill cries, he wanted to cover his ears.

'Mama, wake up! Wake up! They're taking you away!' the

girl screamed madly. Had she not been held back by others, she would have pulled off the sheet. The middle-aged man following the stretcher repeated, sobbing, 'I've let you down! I've let you down!'

His desperate cries were like a knife piercing Fu's heart, as he stared at the stretcher. All of a sudden, as if electrified, he dashed towards his wife's room. He went straight to her, threw himself on the bed. He murmured with closed eyes, 'You're alive!'

Lu stirred, awakened by his heavy breathing. She opened her eyes and looked at him, but her eyes didn't seem to focus.

He felt a shiver of fear and cried out, 'Wenting!'

Her eyes lingered on his face coldly, and this made his heart bleed. Fu did not know what to say or do to encourage her to hold on to life. This was his wife, the dearest person in the world. How long ago was it since he had read poems to her in Beihai Park that winter? During all these years, she had always been his beloved. Life would be unthinkable without her! He must keep her with him!

Poetry! Read a poem to her as he had done then! It was poetry which had helped him to win her before! Today, he would recite her the same poem to remind her of sweet memories, to give her the courage to live on.

Half-kneeling beside her bed, he began to recite with tears in his eyes:

> *'I wish I were a rapid stream,*
> . . . . . .
> *If my love*
> *A tiny fish would be,*
> *She'd frolic*
> *In my foaming waves.'*

The verses seemed to have touched her. She turned her head towards him, her lips moving slightly. Fu leaned over and listened to her indistinct words: 'I can no longer . . . swim. . . .'

Choking back his tears, he continued:

> *'I wish I were a deserted forest,*
> . . . . . .
> *If my love*

> *A little bird would be,*
> *She'd nest and twitter*
> *In my dense trees.'*

She murmured softly, 'I can no longer . . . fly . . .'

His heart ached. Steeling himself, he went on, in tears:

> *'I wish I were a crumbling ruin,*
> *. . . . .*
> *If my love*
> *Green ivy would be,*
> *She'd tenderly entwine*
> *Around my lonely head.'*

Tears, blind tears silently poured down her cheeks and fell on the white pillow. With an effort, she said, 'I can't . . . climb up!'

Fu threw himself on to her, weeping bitterly. 'I've failed you as a husband . . .'

When he opened his tearful eyes, he was astonished. Again she remained with her eyes fixed on the ceiling. She seemed unaware of his weeping, his appeals, unaware of everything around her.

On hearing Fu's sobbing, a doctor hurried in and said to him, 'Dr Lu's very weak. Please don't excite her.'

Fu said nothing more the whole afternoon. At dusk, Lu seemed a little better. She turned her head to Fu and her lips moved as if wanting to speak.

'Wenting, what do you want to say? Tell me,' Fu asked, holding her hands.

She spoke at last, 'Buy Yuanyuan . . . a pair of white gym shoes . . .'

'I'll do it tomorrow,' he replied, unable to check his tears. But he quickly wiped them away with the back of his hand.

Lu, still watching him, seemed to have more to say. But she only uttered a few words after a long time, 'Plait . . . Xiaojia's hair . . .'

'Yes, I will!' Fu promised, still sobbing. He looked at his wife, his vision blurred, hoping she would be able to tell him all that was worrying her. But she closed her lips, as if she had used up her energy.

21

Two days later, a letter came for Lu, posted at Beijing International Airport. Fu opened it and read:

Dear Wenting,

    I wonder if you will ever receive this letter. It's not impossible that this won't reach you. But I hope not! I don't believe it will happen. Though you're very ill, I believe you'll recover. You can still do a lot. You're too young to leave us!

    When my husband and I came to say goodbye to you last night, you were still unconscious. We'd wanted to see you this morning, but there were too many things to do. Yesterday evening we may have met for the last time. Thinking of this, my heart breaks. We've been studying and working together for more than twenty years. No one understands us as well as we do each other. Who would imagine we would part like this?

    I'm now writing this letter in the airport. Can you guess where I'm standing at this moment? At the arts and crafts counter on the second floor. There's no one about, only the shining glass counter in front of me. Remember the first time we travelled by air, we came here too? There was a pot of artificial narcissuses with dew on their petals, so lifelike, so exquisite! You told me that you liked it best. But when we looked at the price, we were scared off. Now, I'm before the counter again, alone, looking at another pot, almost the same colour as the one we saw. Looking at it, I feel like crying. I don't know why. Now I realize suddenly, it's because all that has gone.

    When Fu had just got to know you, I remember once he came to our room and recited a line by Pushkin, 'All that has happened in the past becomes a sweet memory.' I pursed my lips and said it wasn't true. I even asked, 'Can past misfortunes become sweet memories?' Fu grinned, ignoring me. He must have thought inwardly that I knew nothing about poetry. But today I understand. Pushkin was right. It exactly reflects my mood now. It's as if he wrote the line for me! I really feel that all the past is sweet.

A jet has just taken off, its engines roaring. Where is it going? In an hour, I'll be climbing up the steps into the plane, leaving my country. With only sixty minutes to go, I can't help weeping, and my tears wet this letter. But I've no time to rewrite it.

I'm so depressed, I suddenly feel as if I've made the wrong decision. I don't want to leave everything here. No! I can't bear to leave our hospital, our operating theatre, even that little desk in the clinic! I often grumbled that Dr Sun was too severe, never forgiving a mistake. But now I wish I could hear his criticism again. He was a strict teacher. If not for him, I wouldn't be so skilled!

The loudspeakers have just wished passengers bon voyage. Will mine be good? Thinking of boarding the plane in a moment, I feel lost. Where will I land? What lies in store? My heart's in my boots. I'm scared! Yes, scared stiff! Will we get used to a strange country, which is so different from ours? How can my mind be at peace?

My husband's sitting in an armchair brooding. Busy packing the last few days, he had no time to think. He seemed quite firm about the decision. But last night, when he stuffed the last coat into the suitcase, he said all of a sudden, 'We'll be homeless from tomorrow!' He's not spoken since then, and I know his mind is still divided.

Yaya was most happy about this trip. She was nervous and excited, and sometimes I felt like hitting her. But now she's standing at the glass door watching the planes landing and taking off, as if reluctant to leave.

'Won't you change your minds?' you asked that night when we were at your place.

I can't answer that question in one sentence. Liu and I have been discussing it almost every day for the past few months. Our minds have been in a turmoil. There are many reasons, of course, urging us to leave China. It is for Yaya, for Liu and myself. However, none of those reasons can lessen my pain. We shouldn't leave, when China has just begun a new period. We've no excuse for avoiding our duties.

Compared with you, I'm a weak character. Though I had less trouble than you in the past ten years. I couldn't bear it as you did. I often burst out when viciously slandered and attacked. I wasn't as strong as you. On the contrary, it shows my weakness. Better to die than be humiliated, I thought. But there was Yaya. It was surprising that I was able to brazen it out in those days, when Liu was illegally detained as an 'enemy agent'.

All these are bitter memories of the past. Fu was right in saying, 'Darkness has receded, and day has dawned.' The trouble is, the evil influence of many years can't be eradicated overnight. The policies of the government take a long time to reach the people. Resentment is not easily removed. Rumours can kill a person. I dread such a nightmare. I lack your courage!

I remember that you and I were cited at that meeting as bourgeois specialists. When we left the hospital afterwards, I said to you, 'I can't understand all this. Why should people who have worked hard in their field be crushed? I'll refuse to attend such meetings as a protest!' But you said, 'Forget it! If they want to hold a hundred such meetings, let them. I'll attend. We'll still have to do the operations. I'll study at home.' I asked you, 'Don't you feel wronged?' You smiled and said, 'I'm so busy, I've not time to care.' I admired you very much. Before we parted, you warned me, 'Don't tell Fu about such things. He's in enough trouble himself.' We walked a block in silence. I noticed that you looked very calm, very confident. No one could shake your faith. I knew that you had a strong will, which enabled you to resist all kinds of attacks and go your own way. If I had half your courage and will-power, I wouldn't have made such a decision.

Forgive me! This is all I can say to you now. I'm leaving, but I'm leaving my heart with you, with my dear homeland. Wherever I go, I'll never forget China. Believe me! Believe that I'll return. After a few years, when Yaya's grown up and we have achieved something in medicine, we'll come back.

I hope you'll soon recover! Learn a lesson from your illness and pay more attention to your health. I'm not advising you to be selfish. I've always admired your selflessness. I wish you good health to make full use of your talents!

Goodbye, my dearest friend!

Affectionately,
Yafen

22

A month and a half later, Dr Lu had basically recovered and was permitted to go home.

It was a miracle. Ill as she was, Lu, several times on the brink of death, survived. The doctors were greatly surprised and delighted.

That morning, Fu jubilantly helped her put on a cotton-padded jacket, a pair of woollen trousers, a blue overcoat, and wrapped around her neck a long fluffy beige scarf.

'How are things at home?' she asked.

'Fine. The comrades of your Party branch came yesterday to help clean the room.'

Her thoughts immediately turned to that small room with the large bookcase covered with a white cloth, the little alarm-clock on the window-sill and the desk . . .

She felt feeble and cold, though so warmly dressed. Her legs trembled when she stood up. With one hand gripping her husband's arm, the other touching the wall, she moved forward leaning heavily on Fu. Slowly, she walked out of the ward.

Zhao, Sun and her other colleagues followed her, watching her progress along the corridor towards the gate.

It had rained for a couple of days. A gust of wind sighed through the bare branches of the trees. The sunshine, extraordinarily bright after the rain, slanted in through the windows of the corridor. The cold wind blew in too. Slowly Fu, supporting his wife, headed for the sunlight and the wind.

A black car was waiting at the steps. It had been sent by the administration department at Zhao's request.

Leaning on her husband's shoulder, Lu walked slowly towards the gate . . .

Translated by Yu Fanqin and Wang Mingjie

Jiang Zilong

Jiang Zilong is known for his controversial short stories that deal with life in the factories. His output has been small but his works have won him considerable acclaim and attention. Attention that during the period of cultural restriction could better be called notoriety. He is a northern writer and was born in 1941 in Hebei, the province in which Beijing is located. His background is very diverse. Initially he had set his heart on becoming a mechanical engineer and attended a technical school in Tianjin in 1950 but was forced to give up his studies and take up an apprenticeship because his family was so poor. He was then conscripted into the navy and during his five years of service was given the opportunity to learn cartography. On completing his training he was employed in a heavy engineering plant in Tianjin as a blacksmith. He rose to positions of political and administrative responsibility such as Secretary and Deputy Workshop Director.

His interest in writing had been awakened while still in the navy with the publication in the Navy newspaper of a set piece of so-called 'reportage' on 'the model soldier'.

His career as an amateur writer really began with the publication in 1956 of his first short story. Subsequent stories appearing at the end of the Cultural Revolution and afterwards aroused heated controversy. *A Day in the Life of the Director of the Mechanical and Electrical Bureau*, published in 1976, attracted criticism for putting forward a theory of productive forces to the exclusion of all else. The short story *Factory Manager Qiao Takes Up His Post* (1979) had his critics divided into those who objected to it fiercely and those who approved. Jiang Zilong's own comment on the fuss it was causing was:

> Each time one of my few works appear I attract criticism. Some even suggest that I should make a clean break from writing altogether. On occasions I have contemplated giving it up, but my sense of responsibility would not allow it.

He is also one of the few writers who has described briefly what the writing process means to him. He says that for him it is dogged hard work. His subject matter, his characters, any good plots or particularly apt details of the writing have never just come to him by happy accident, they have all been drawn from his experience of life at first hand.

The story in this anthology *Pages from a Factory Secretary's Diary* was published in the Tianjin journal *The New Harbour* (Number 5, 1980). In the words of a critic from *Chinese Literature* 'A prominent characteristic of his writing over the last few years has been criticism of the excessive bureaucratism and the anarchy prevalent during the ten years of the Cultural Revolution. Moreover, certain suggested methods of solution are implicit in what he has written.'

Jiang Zilong
Pages from a Factory Secretary's Diary

4 March 1979

I went to the factory an hour earlier than usual today because I wanted to say goodbye to Manager Wang, who was leaving for good. I reckoned that a man like him wouldn't kick up a fuss about it but would go quietly before the workers arrived.

Wang himself had asked for the transfer, but in fact, I'm pretty sure, he felt unable to continue working in this factory. He was simply squeezed out by Assistant Manager Luo Ming. It was an open secret, yet people kept mum, especially in front of Wang. No one would rub it in. It was really awful.

As a factory secretary for four years, I've seen off two managers. Now Wang is the third.

When something is wrong with the management in a factory, a transfer is the most convenient remedy. That's probably true everywhere. Each time I say goodbye to a manager, I examine myself. It takes me a week to get over it.

I decided to use my power for the first time to order our only jeep to take Wang to his new place.

But a janitor told me that he had left half an hour before!

'All on his own?' I asked.

'Party Secretary Liu carried his luggage for him.'

'But where's our jeep?'

'Luo had it out on business last night.'

I was very upset. I'd hoped to get to the factory to give Wang a hand. But obviously the man behind all this dirty business had pipped me at the post.

I had a sudden feeling of resentment against Liu, the number one in our factory. What a weakling! Shandong, his home province, has been famous for its heroes since ancient days. Where were his guts? Numbers one and two squeezing into a bus with all that luggage!

As I was musing, the jeep sped in in a cloud of dust. Luo got out, beaming.

'Hello, Wei!' he said in a mocking tone. 'Why so early? Seeing Wang off? Has he left?'

'Yes.'

I'm laconic, especially when I'm in a bad mood. The least said, the soonest mended! A secretary must watch his tongue. A blunder can bring a lot of trouble.

Luo fumbled in his pocket and fished out a few fire-crackers. Passing them to me, he said, 'have some fun!'

Refusing to take them, I replied, 'I don't dare light them.'

He snorted, 'You're no man!'

'You often carry them in your pockets?'

'Left-overs from the Spring Festival. I'll set them all off and clear the air!'

Crack! He lit one and guffawed.

A cold shiver went down my spine. Wang was lucky to have left already. How would he have felt about this?

Manager—a post which is so enticing to certain people! In an attempt to remove the word 'assistant' in his title, Lou had pushed out three men. But twice new managers had been appointed. Will another come or will Luo be promoted? If the latter, I'll have to consider leaving too, quitting the manager's office and going back to the production department to work on statistics again.

March 11

'Wei, have you heard that Luo's been made manager?' Quite a number of workers tried to sound me out.

'No, I haven't.' My answer was the same.

Then someone would probe, 'Oh, come off it! Surely you've heard it.'

Poor fellows! Having no say whatever in the factory, yet wanting to know everything. Pointless curiosity! No matter who's the manager, you'll have to work all the same. It's none of your business!

'Manager Luo, you're wanted on the phone!' People have begun to address him like this these days. Even some workshop reports start with 'Manager Luo'. 'Assistant' has been omitted. Those cunning cadres, who have already trimmed their sails to suit the wind, are more pitiful than the workers.

'Wei, don't you smell a rat? Luo works hard these days. He's got a finger in every pie. He's all over the place. Always with a smile on his face. Even his voice is louder.'

'No, I don't.' You're here to work, I thought, not to watch others' expressions. Perhaps it's my professional weakness, my nerves have gone dull or numb. I've got used to all kinds of speeches and facial expressions. I take nothing to heart.

Since I know there are some who watch my expressions and weigh my words carefully, when I have to address Luo, I always take the trouble to say his full title—'Assistant Manager Luo'.

When certain documents require a manager's perusal, I give them to Liu, the Party branch secretary, according to the rules. I then pass them on to whoever he tells me. I don't intend to flatter Luo. He's probably sensed it. However, since I haven't been officially informed about the promotion, he can't do anything about it.

I don't care whether or not he's going to be the manager. That's none of my business. If the higher-ups ask my opinion, I'll object. He's been in this factory for ages, knows everything about it and he has quite a following, yet he'll never be a good manager. All he cares about is power, not responsibility. He lacks the necessary qualities and ability to be a good manager.

March 12

It's strange. Luo's daughter, Luo Jingyu, came to my office and chatted for some time.

She's been job-hunting since she came back from the countryside two years ago. The trouble is, she's too choosy. She won't work in a collective-owned factory, nor in a job she doesn't like and she refuses to go somewhere a bit far from home. As she rarely comes to our factory, I couldn't work out at first what she was up to, yacking away in the office. Then she mentioned the question of her job at last and said, 'I want to work here.'

'You must be kidding!' I said doubtfully. 'Though we're state-owned, we're small, only two hundred people. Nothing to write home about. Besides, there's no job you'd fancy here.'

'It's difficult to get a good job, and I've been waiting for two years.' She told the truth. 'I'm already twenty-six. I can't afford to wait any more. A chemical factory has its advantages. The production costs are low, but the profit's great. So your bonuses are high.'

'That's quite true. Have a word with your father then.'

'He would find it embarrassing to help me. Wei, will you do me a favour?'

Here was an opportunity for a man who wanted to butter up his superior and climb up the social ladder. If it was inconvenient for a manager to do something, then it was up to his secretary to help him out. He should run errands and do the job in all kinds of names if necessary to achieve his superior's aims.

When I had failed to resist the Party branch committee's decision to appoint me as the factory secretary, I made a rule for myself that there would be nothing personal between my superiors and me. No matter who he was, our relationship was strictly business! Public affairs should be conducted in an orthodox way. Personal considerations shouldn't intrude.

'Wait till I ask the Party branch committee,' I replied.

She was totally unprepared for such an answer. She thought that, as she was the daughter of the manager and I was her father's secretary, I should naturally serve her too. She was very cross and, after a snigger which was just like her father's, left with a slam of the door.

15 March

'Our new manager will come soon,' Secretary Liu told me jovially in a low voice.

This down-to-earth man was as innocent as a lamb. He had received three managers in the same jovial mood and sulkily seen them off, carrying their bags. Today he was again in high spirits.

I was neither very happy nor disappointed. I was simply bored.

18 March

The telephone in the office kept ringing. I heard it from quite far away. People mock those who enter the factory gate just as the bell is ringing. But I enter the office five days out of six just as the phone is ringing.

Calls at this time are usually for managers. It is the right time to catch them. Half an hour later and they're nowhere to be found. Even I have no idea of their whereabouts, let alone what they are busy with.

Brr. . .

As a secretary, I was used to it. No matter how urgent it sounds, I am never in a hurry. I opened the door, hung up my bag, had a bite of my bun and finally picked up the receiver.

'Hello! Is that Secretary Wei? Would you do me a favour, Wei? My father died yesterday and he's to be cremated today. Could you have a word with the manager and say that I want to borrow a car? Do help me out, please!'

Startled, I inquired, 'Who is it?'

'This is Pang. Pang Wancheng. Sorry to trouble you.'

'Why didn't you let me know earlier?' I complained.

'How could I know he would die so soon?'

I was hard put to it. 'You know that we've only one jeep and one lorry. But they went to fetch raw materials from the countryside yesterday. They won't be back for a day or two. What can I do?'

Pang was a very simple, honest crane-operator and he would never ask the factory for help if he wasn't desperate. Despite what I told him, he stubbonly continued pleading, 'Wei, I'm in no position to ask Manager Luo for such a favour. But you've been a secretary for years. You know much better than me how to solve the problem. I've no one to turn to. The time for the cremation has been fixed. All our relatives will come soon. What shall I do if I can't get a car?'

In the eyes of the workers, I seem to be a man of power too. They don't realize I'm just the manager's errand-boy and mouthpiece. However, I couldn't explain that to him at that moment. It seemed that I was the only 'important person' he knew, his last hope.

While I was still talking, a stout, short fellow suddenly appeared behind me and said smilingly, 'Let me speak to him.'

Astonished, I asked, 'What—what are you doing here?'

This bloke had a charming round face with a pair of big sparkling eyes.

He looked like a salesman from a factory who had come on business. Pointing, I said, 'The production department's the third room on the left.'

He shook his head and introduced himself, 'My names's Jin Fengchi. I have been sent by the Bureau of Chemical Industry to work here.'

The new manager! My heart missed a beat.

I cursed myself. A secretary shouldn't be so snobbish. Why did I judge a man by his appearance?

I handed him the phone. When he spoke, his voice became serious and concerned, 'Don't worry, Comrade Pang. Tell me, when do you need a car?'

He took a biro from his breast pocket and I gave him a piece of paper. While repeating Pang's words, he scribbled on the paper. 'Ten o'clock, fine. Your address? No. 8, Fifth Lane, Jinzhou Street. Good. What's your name again? Pang Wancheng. OK, Wancheng, wait at home and I'll send you a van. Don't be so polite. Anything else I can do for you? My name isn't important. Anyway you can stop worrying now. But don't be too upset. Better take care of yourself. Have a few days off and rest.'

He rang off. Taking the receiver in his left hand, he dialled a number. 'Is that the Chemical Machinery Repair Plant? Who's speaking? Du! Guess who's speaking to you? Ha! Ha! . . . Yes, I'm in my new job. No choice. Very sad to leave you and our factory too. Look, I've a slight problem here. Can I borrow your van? Excellent! Ten o'clock. Tell Young Sun to go to No. 8, Fifth Lane, Jinzhou Street and look for a man named Pang

Wancheng. Sorry to trouble you. Phone me whenever you want me.'

Having put down the receiver, he turned to ask me, 'How many telephones do we have?'

'Ours is a small factory, so there are only three. There's one here, one in the production department and another in the reception office.'

Pulling over a stool and sitting down, he produced a cigarette case and handed me a cigarette. Having lit his, he said slowly, 'Surely you must be Secretary Wei, a very capable man I hear.'

'My name's Wei Jixiang. I'm a square peg in a round hole, not really qualified.'

I wanted to impress on him that I had no interest in my present job.

'I'm new here,' he said politely. 'I need your help.'

I quickly waved my hands to show I could do very little.

His face fell. 'I'm not being polite,' he said seriously. 'Cadres learn from the people and a manager from his secretary. It's the secretary who drafts the manager's speech for mass meetings. All a manager does is to read it aloud from the platform. A manager's competence largely depends on his secretary's level. If the secretary's lousy, the manager probably won't be any good either. You read all the documents first and then pass them on to the managers concerned. Besides, you have to attend to the managers' odd jobs. Managers may be the leaders of the factory, but you're their boss.'

I was fidgeting, feeling, in turn, comfortable and uneasy. My face was burning. I couldn't figure out whether he was flattering me or being sarcastic. I am considered a man with some education in the factory. But today I was all at sea, unable to tell whether or not he was serious.

It is too early to jump to conclusions, but one thing is certain, he's no fool!

At noon, Pang came straight from the crematorium and asked me to take him to the new manager.

Secretary Liu was showing Jin round the workshops as Pang, a black band round his arm, and I searched everwhere for him. Not knowing what had happened, many people followed us.

On seeing Jin, Pang went over and kowtowed in the traditional way. I was shocked!

Jin was surprised too. He hurriedly helped him up and said, 'Comrade Pang, what on earth are you doing?'

Pang was very grateful to him. Too emotional, he stuttered when he spoke, 'A th-th-thousand thanks, M-M-Manager Jin. If you hadn't sent the van, goodness knows how long my father's body would have remained at home. He'll be grateful to you too in the nether world. Thank you very much.'

Jin wanted to pat him on the shoulder to comfort him but he was too short. So he gripped Pang's arm instead and said earnestly, 'Don't talk like that, Pang. Nowadays those who have influential connections use them. Those who have power use it. But what about the workers who have neither? We can't blame the workers for their resentment, nor can we complain that they are less enthusiastic than before 1958. We can't say that they're selfish and only thinking of themselves. If nobody seems to care about them, they have to look after themselves.' I was flabbergasted. He was really bold to talk like that! Though new, he seemed very frank with the workers. He talked in a way as if he were defending them.

What he said touched their hearts. The admiration in their eyes and their whispered comments showed that his words were more effective than an 'inaugral address' at a mass meeting.

Liu was delighted to see the workers responding positively to the new manager and said earnestly to Jin, 'The workers of this factory are a fine lot, aren't they? They like you.'

Jin turned to Pang and continued, 'Wancheng, your father's dead now, but don't let it get you down too much. Take a few days off. You must look after yourself too.'

He had said that over the phone and now he was repeating himself in public.

Deeply moved, Pang didn't know what to say. Flushing, he replied, 'No. I won't have a rest. I'll come back to work today.'

Having said that, he began to put on his overalls. He had

only taken half of his three days' leave for the funeral.

Liu led the manager to another workshop. As I turned to go to my office, I spotted Luo standing at the back of the crowd. Gazing after the two receding figures of Liu and Jin, he puffed vigorously on his cigarette. The pale pock-marks on his face became more distinct, an indicator of his feelings. When he was in high spirits, they disappeared. When he was furious, his red face seemed to make the marks whiter.

He went to Pang and said smilingly, 'Pang Wancheng, I never thought that a big man like you could be so yellow-bellied! So a van can make you grovel on your knees!'

Unprepared for this, Pang stammered, 'Manager Luo, you're . . .'

Luo is a ruthless man, liable to get nasty any minute. Very often, he would suddenly scold for no obvious reasons. I pretended not to have seen them and went to the office.

But he caught me up and walked abreast with me.

'Wei,' he spoke up, 'our new chief certainly knows how to win friends and influence people!'

I said nothing. I've always avoided rivalry between managers. I'm impartial to all.

But no doubt our little factory will soon have troubles again.

23 March

'The first thing Manager Jin did was to borrow a van from outside for the most honest worker of our factory.'

The news soon got around. After much exaggeration, it assumed an air of romance.

How easily people are satisfied and moved!

2 April

Manager Jin and I got into the jeep and went to the company to report on our work. However, neither of us spoke for some time.

But suddenly he asked me a very peculiar question, ' "I may be a dragon here, but I'll be no match for you, a snake in its old haunts." Do you know which opera that line is from?'

'*Shajiabang*,' I said, throwing him a glance.

Another silence. But I understand perfectly what he meant.

It was not until we got out and entered the office block of the company, he ventured again, 'We must speak first. At the beginning, people tend to be formal and the big shots would like to listen to others first. So it's an opportunity for a small factory like ours. Besides, at the start of the meeting, leading comrades are attentive and listen carefully. But later their concentration wanes. They'll begin smoking, drinking tea or going to the lavatory. No one will be really listening.'

He was sharp. But I was still worried. What had he got to say? He'd been in the factory less than a month!

The company had notified us that there would be a managers' meeting. Liu, thinking Jin was far too new, suggested that Luo attend the meeting. I knew Luo liked to appear on such occasions. But Jin smiled and said, 'Better for me to go.' It was very subtle. Was he against letting Luo attend the meeting as a manager or was he eager to seek the limelight himself?

Sure enough, as the meeting was declared open, he spoke first. He was eloquent and his example of Pang only taking half of his three days' leave was vivid and moving. While he commended the workers, he impressed the listeners with his art of leadership.

We were praised at the meeting, unusual for a tiny factory like ours.

I felt more and more that Jin was not as simple as he seemed.

When the second man began his report, Jin whispered to me, 'Jot down the good points, Wei, particularly others' experiences and the company directors' instructions. I'm going out for a moment.'

He was away for several hours, only reappearing shortly before the meeting ended. Very strange!

25 April

It gets more and more peculiar. The marks on Luo's face are less visible. Has the power struggle come to an end? Luo is not a man to easily knuckle under. Has he thrown up the sponge? Not likely!

When I entered the office at noon after lunch, I saw Jin talking over the phone, Luo beside him, wearing an obsequious look, which was very rare.

'. . . Her name's Luo Jingyu, a relative of mine. You must help her however difficult. I'll expect your answer within a week. OK. So it's settled?'

The penny dropped. I have no admiration for Jin's way of doing things, but I have to admit that he certainly has a good head on his shoulders. Luo is a difficult man to co-operate with, but he knows thoroughly our production and has quite a following. If he is under Jin's thumb, Jin can consider himself really settled in the factory.

But I had never expected that Jin would do such a thing. He certainly knows how to win over a philistine. No wonder people remark behind his back that he is as slick as a snake.

10 May

Jin and I went to a meeting at the bureau. Not long after it had started, he again whispered to me, 'Keep notes, Wei. I'll be out for a moment.

Whenever we had meetings either in the company or the bureau, he always played the same trick. What on earth did he go out for? What could keep him that busy?

After a short while I left the meeting room. It was quite warm and many offices had their doors open. As I went up to the second floor, I happened to see Jin wandering from room to room. He seemed to have dropped in to have a chat or a laugh with practically everybody from the department heads to staff members. He had brought with him plenty of good cigarettes and offered them generously to everyone who smoked. But it was not just one-sided, he was given cigarettes too. He was very familiar with the people working there. Drinking and smoking, he was utterly at ease. Sometimes he had business to do, sometimes he came just to chat. A couple of hours were easily killed this way.

Our factory is a tiny unit in the Bureau of Chemical Industry. That a manager of such a factory is on good terms with many people including some cadres higher than himself in the bureau is really something remarkable!

On the way back to our factory after the meeting, I told him, 'I hear you've got a lot of friends in the bureau.'

'Didn't you realize that this afternoon?' He grinned at me.

I couldn't cover up my embarrassment.

'Wei,' he said buoyantly, 'we've been together for some time now, and I've come to know that you're a very good comrade. Your handwriting's absolutely beautiful and you write quickly. Day after day, you run your legs off, working harder than any manager. However, I must say, you're a bit of a stick-in-the-mud. Tell you what, in capitalist countries, money counts, but in our country, it's your connections. That's something I've learned through experience. This certainly won't change in the next three to five years. Ours is a small factory and we've no big cadres. That means we've neither power nor position. If you don't have good connections and don't butter people up, you can do nothing.'

An amazing theory! I could not decide if he was admirable or despicable.

12 May

Luo was all smiles when he spoke to me in a cheerful voice, 'Wei, I've got a job for you. Will you bring Manager Jin to my home for dinner tonight? He probably won't come alone, so I'm roping you in too. Do everything you can to persuade him.'

'Toadying to the boss!' I thought. 'So humble, just because he's found your daughter a job.'

But what else could I expect of someone who had been a pump-keeper, then joined the Party and become an assistant manager by chance? I'd never have dinner in his home! In the past, I always made some excuse. 'Just my luck!' I said. 'My son's got pneumonia! I'll have to take him to hospital after work today.'

His face darkened at once. 'I suppose I'm not important enough! Well, don't trouble then. Just send Jin to my home OK?'

What could I do? I was a factory secretary after all. Gazing after his back, I cursed, 'I'll be damned if I'll let my son be a secretary!'

I went to Jin when it was time to knock off. He accepted the invitation bluntly and urged me to accept. I told the same lie again. Narrowing his eyes, he grinned and said, 'Don't make it up, Wei. You're no good at lying. Your face gives you away!'

'But it's true, every word!' I defended myself hastily.

'Oh, come off it!' he guffawed. 'You don't even bother to change your lies! Always the same story. Your little fib is known all over the factory. People say, "When Wei doesn't want to go somewhere, he excuses himself by making his wife or children ill." You're an educated man. Can't you invent some other story?'

I shook my head, smiling wrily.

Patting me on the shoulder, he continued, 'You poor innocent! The assistant manager is throwing a dinner for us. That's our good luck, you know. I won't take a sip of any liquor under two yuan a bottle! Come with me. You don't have to say a word, just eat your fill! Isn't it great?'

I didn't go anyway. But I learned that Luo's daughter had started work in a state-owned radio factory today. So that was why Luo threw the dinner. Jin is really quite a character to have tamed a fellow like Luo.

When the Party spirit, discipline and laws don't work for someone, personal feelings and favouritism may have their place.

But I'm unimpressed by Jin's way of doing things. In fact, his simplicity and kindness, which made such an impression on me the first day he arrived, have changed.

(*Diary entries from June to September are omitted here.*)

9 October

The complications among the leading comrades reflect those in society and people's thinking.

Now Luo and Jin have ganged up, while there's a growing tension between Jin and Liu. This morning, there was the inevitable show-down over bonuses at the Party branch committee meeting.

A government document circulated in September said that a factory was entitled to bonuses proportionate to its profits. The raw material our factory needs is others' waste material. The capital is small, but the profit remarkable. As a rule, the smaller the number of workers in a factory, the easier the bonus is given. It was calculated at the end of September that each worker could get a fifty-yuan bonus and an office worker more than forty. That meant most of the workers would get double their rate of pay.

Being an honest and straightforward man, Liu was astonished to hear this. Forty yuan a month extra was, of course, something he needed, for his living standard was the lowest among the top leaders of the factory. But he was against it. Shaking his head, he protested, 'That won't do! Such a big bonus? Out of the question!'

'What's there to be afraid of?' many workers countered, disappointment showing on their faces. Everybody welcomed having some extra cash. But the members of the Party branch committee sat on the fence, staring at the manager and the Party secretary, waiting for a decision. They wanted the money but were hesitant about bearing the responsibility.

'Speak your mind, Luo,' Jin urged the assistant manager.

Luo was very blunt, 'Give the bonus to the workers. Act according to the document.'

Liu retorted, 'The document applies to enterprises in general. But ours is an exception. We can't take advantage of this. We must thoroughly understand the spirit of the document. Besides, the leaders might not approve of it if they knew.'

'What would you do with the money?' Luo asked. 'Hand it over to the state for nothing?'

'Put it in the bank for the time being. It'll come in handy for the community welfare fund.'

Silently Jin smoked. No one knew what he was thinking. He is expert in handling people, always weighing the pros and cons carefully. He would never risk his position for a few dozen yuan for the workers. What if he should offend the company or the bureau? Surely he knew which side to back. He would never lose a lot to save a little. Besides, the Party secretary had already made his attitude clear. He wouldn't oppose Liu.

I thought too that Jin would surely be against the large bonus.

As I'd expected, Jin said, 'Liu's right. The sum's a bit on the large side . . .'

'You—' Luo uttered, his face suddenly red.

Jin wagged his finger at him, as if there had been an agreement between them. I realized all of a sudden that Jin was making use of Luo, a headstrong fellow, to sound out Liu first.

Jin continued, 'We're the leaders of the Oriental Chemical Factory. We needn't worry about the state. Our chief concern is the welfare of the workers of this factory. If we offend them, we'll certainly get into trouble. We've read the document to the workers. If we don't issue the bonus according to the document, we'll be breaking our promise and damaging the image of the state. It'll put us in a bad light for sure. Even worse, the workers will be disheartened, and production will drop. So I vote for giving the bonus, every cent of it. If the company inquires into it, we can say we were carrying out the instructions in the document. If other factories raise questions and poke their noses into our affairs, we'll tell them we acted according to the principle of "more pay for more work". Our factory's doing well. We've made a good profit for the state. Of course we're entitled to a big bonus. Now what do you think?'

As most of the members agreed with what he'd said, it was decided thus. Liu felt it wrong to give such a big bonus, but he had no convincing argument. Though it was a majority vote, he was still uneasy. He asked Jin to stay behind after the meeting.

Work had already ended, but I didn't go home since I still had some urgent business to attend to. The window above the door leading to Liu's office was open. While writing, I could hear clearly the conversation in Liu's room. I am worried about him. He is too old-fashioned, too inflexible. In the past, he'd been fretting a great deal about the friction between the manager and the assistant manager. Wang had suited him very well, a decent and upright man, honest and frank to both his inferiors and superiors. But he was narrow-minded, and often sulked. He couldn't brazen it out and finally left after less than a year in the job. Jin is shrewd and able and hits it off well with everybody. Even Luo has succumbed and co-operates with him. Liu should be having an easy life. Yet he goes looking for trouble. In the past, he and Wang had failed to contain Luo. How can he now deal with Jin and Luo single-handed?

Liu's voice in the next room became louder and louder. . . To be a leader, one must play fair. It's wrong to pander to one faction or try to please everybody. What's worse is to curry favour by giving away the state's money. Jin, some people have complained to me about you. You ought to watch your step.'

It was terrible. How could a Party secretary speak to a manager like that? To ease the tension, I hurriedly sent them the material I'd just written.

Jin was really smart. He listened with patience, no sign of anger on his face. Seeing me, he smiled and remarked, 'You've come at the right time, Wei. Let's talk it over together. This Party secretary of ours is really impossible! No wonder the leading body of this factory was so ineffective and always at odds with each other. Instead of helping his subordinates out of difficulties, he needs them to help him out. Now tell me, Liu, how am I not playing fair? You accuse me of currying favour by giving away the state's money, but didn't I do it according to the spirit of the document?'

Liu sighed, waving his hand and replied, 'As for money, the more the better. I know the workers won't be very happy if we lessen the bonus. But as leaders, we must think about their long-term interests. We must guide them, educate them. Doesn't the document also say that part of the bonus can be used for the community welfare fund?'

'If you hold back the fifty yuan, you'll enrage the workers. What exactly do you want that money for?'

'For some future use. For instance, we must ensure that we can give a bonus every month, no matter how small. Even if we fail in fulfilling the production quota, we can still give a bonus, just in case. Besides, if we've put aside enough money, we can build a few more houses for the workers.'

'Forget it, Liu! Haven't you had enough?' Jin then turned to me, 'As a secretary, Wei, you must have learned this lesson.

Act promptly while you've power in your hands. The document says you can give the bonus, so give it! If you hesitate now, you can do nothing about the money later if the directive is changed. As for the housing problem, I tell you frankly, it won't be easy to build a dozen houses for a small factory like ours. The construction departments will want a couple of them when the houses are put up. Then there are those in charge of electricity, water, coal and even food stores. . . How many rooms will be left for us? You'll spend the money, sweat over it, and then what will you get in return? Troubles, abuse! What benefit will the workers of this factory really get? Better put a lump sum in their hands!'

Though Liu didn't quite agree, he said nothing more.

Jin offered us cigarettes, but Liu refused. Instead, he took out his own. Jin wasn't offended, lighting a cigarette himself. Drawing on it deeply, he continued, 'Liu, the way you handle things was OK before 1958, but it won't work now. Take the document. Abide by it, but don't be too strict. There's a lot to learn. For example, how many times have you got yourself in a fix? Those who had been sent to the countryside during the Cultural Revolution were allowed to come back to town and were allocated jobs. But you didn't act quickly enough, and it was soon stopped. You lost the opportunity and everyone was mad at you. Then all those whose wages had been frozen were to be refunded. Those who got in first were lucky. Those who were slow got nothing. There are lots of examples. If you're inflexible, you'll lose every chance.'

Jin hoped sincerely that Liu would change a bit. But I think Liu was disgusted by his theory.

10 October

The bonus was issued, and everybody talked about it. What upset me was that they seemed to know all the gory details about the disagreement the previous day, even better than my minutes! Liu became the target of all their gripes, while Jin was worshipped as a hero.

It is unfair to put Liu in such a bad light.

Jin decided to hold a mass meeting to mobilize the workers at this favourable time. At the meeting, he made a short yet moving speech. There was no draft, but he knew what he was talking about.

'All the bonus is given to you, every bit of it. Some people were shocked at such a big sum. Frankly, if we work harder, our profit will rise even more, and next month you'll probably get an even bigger bonus. So long as I'm in charge of the money, I assure you that all that you're entitled to will be given to you without delay, without a cent deducted!'

2 November

It was just my day! From early dawn till mid afternoon, I only caught a couple of small carp. On my way home, I ran into Jin. He'd got a crateful, so I asked where he had been fishing. Instead of replying, he smiled. I reckoned that he must have known the keeper and had fished in his pond. Despite my refusal, he gave me half his fish. When I passed his home, he invited me in. It was difficult to refuse. Besides, I wanted to have a look at his home. A capable man like him, I guessed, must have a nice flat with fashionable furniture. But to my surprise, it was so simple that I could hardly believe it was his.

He asked his daughter, who was doing her homework, to cook, while he offered me a drink. Glowering at him, the girl took up her satchel and went into her granny's room.

So he had to turn to his mother. Reluctantly, the old woman went to the kitchen grumbling. I soon learned why from her complaints.

Jin earned seventy yuan a month, but he only contributed a little for the house-keeping. He smoked good cigarettes and drank good alcohol. Every evening after work, he boozed. When he got home, he made do with a snack. So his wife had to keep his mother and the two children on her salary.

He was no boss at home, not like in the factory.

I had not imagined Jin was such a bloke.

31 December

The bell had long since rung but the cadres still stayed in the factory at the request of Jin, who had phoned from the bank. The bonus for each worker at the end of the year was a hundred yuan. However, the bank refused to pay the money. Jin had gone to the bank, taking with him the document. Trying to persuade them to agree, he had stayed there for a whole day, not even returning for lunch, but no one knew why he asked the cadres to wait for him.

He returned at last. Elated, he told the cadres, 'Make it snappy, everybody! We must divide the money and give it to the workers today.'

Overjoyed, everyone was raring to go. Under the direction of the head of the financial department, they put into each red envelope a hundred yuan.

Liu called Jin to my office and said emotionally, 'Jin, we can't do this. It's all wrong to give bonuses at random! It's not stated in the document that the workers should be given a big sum at the end of the year, is it?'

'But it doesn't say we shouldn't either, does it?' Jin was edgy after a hard day.

'Jin, it's a mistake. We're not going to close down after the New Year, are we?'

'Oh you! You're impossible!' he snapped, barely concealing his irritation. 'How many times have I told you that we must give all the bonus to the workers? And we must do it today. Or why did I waste my time at the bank? The higher-ups keep changing their minds. Who can predict the new rule next year? If a new document comes freezing bonuses, then we'll be in trouble! The workers will be furious with us.'

'Don't worry! I'll answer for it!'

'But it's been decided at the Party branch committee meeting. You can't change it now.' Jin pushed open the door and left. This was the first time I had seen him in a rage.

3 January 1980

As soon as I began work today I received several documents, one of which stated that all the 1979 bonuses were frozen.

I showed it to Jin. He chuckled and said, 'I knew it would happen.'

When it was read among the workers, they felt all the more grateful to the manager. Even the cadres couldn't help talking about it. It was really lucky! One day's delay and the bonuses would have been lost. Our manager was a man of vision and action!

This afternoon, we elected a delegate to the People's Congress. The candidate was chosen by the workers themselves this time. It was really democratic. The whole factory was divided into five groups: four workshops and one group of cadres. Jin won the election by an overwhelming majority in the three workshops. He almost got full votes in the cadres' group except three. It had been expected. But one person from the fourth workshop wrote on his voting slip, 'Jin Fengchi is an old fox!'

The workers, who were chosen to count the ballot, told someone about this, and it was a blow to Jin's pride.

After work, Jin came to me, a bottle of alcohol in his hand. 'Don't go, Wei,' he said. 'Have pity on a homeless man! Have a drink with me.'

He produced some peanuts from his pocket.

'Why don't you go home?' I asked.

'My wife and I had a quarrel last night. I can't go home today, or we'll fight again.' He poured himself a drink and gulped it down.

'Jin, you ought to look after your family,' I chaffed. 'From next month, I'll take most of your salary to them.'

He smiled. 'Chin-chin! Even an upright official finds it hard to settle a family quarrel. We've been at odds for twenty years, and she can never get the better of me. You want to try? Cheers!'

He drank like a fish. There was nothing to eat except the peanuts, which he nibbled. Before long, his eyes became bloodshot.

He stared at me and remarked all of a sudden, 'It's very difficult to please people nowadays. They're a mixture of any and every sort. No matter how hard you try, somebody's always grousing.'

I knew what he meant. But it was hard for me to say anything. He had another sip and continued, 'I've offended the Party secretary in the interest of the workers. If I'd pleased the Party secretary, I'd have offended the workers. Do you know who cast the three votes against me?'

I was startled. How could he know who voted against him? He must have suspected Liu. But Liu was open and obviously wouldn't vote for him.

'I don't know,' was all I could say.

'Luo's one of them. No question!'

I was so shocked, I could hardly believe it. 'But he admires you a lot, doesn't he?'

He grinned. 'I did him a favour. Anyway, his little tricks can never fool me. He's a ruthless character and very ambitious. But he was right not to vote for me.'

'What about the third one?'

Pointing at himself, he said, 'That was mine.'

He was either drunk or making fun of me.

'It's true,' he said, tossing down his drink. Now the liquor had really gone to his head. 'I know you must think that I'm as slick as a snake. But I wasn't born like that. The longer you muddle along in this society, the smarter you become. After a few slips and falls even you'd wise up. The more complex the society, the sharper the people. Liu's a good man, but he didn't get as many votes as I. How can good men like him cope in future? If I'd listened to Liu and run the factory in a rigid way, production would have dropped. I'd have offended the workers and there'd be no profit. The state and our leaders wouldn't have been happy about it. Don't think I'm glad because I've got most votes. On the contrary, I feel very bad. I knew Liu wouldn't vote for me, but I voted for him . . .'

'You're a bit tipsy, Jin,' I said, helping him to a bed which was for those on night duty. 'Have a rest. I'll go home and fetch you some food.'

I deeply regretted that I'd voted in his favour. Though he got most votes, he is not of the calibre of a people's delegate, even in these times.

I'm certain that he'll lose the next election.

Translated by Wang Mingjie

Zhang Lin

Zhang Lin, the author of this very short but poignant story, *The Stranger*, like Li Huiwen, is Manchurian. He was also born in Liaoning, in 1939. Zhang Lin has a higher level of formal education than most of these authors. After completing secondary school he studied at the Harbin College of Art. He did not make a living from his art, however, but worked in the railways as an attendant from 1961, then became head of a train crew and is now in charge of the railway team. He began writing as an amateur pursuit in 1973 and had some of his stories and novellas published. His short story *Are You a Communist Party Member?* won a Category Two prize in the 1980 awards for the best short stories. *The Stranger*, published in the Heilongjiang journal *Northern Literature*, No. 1, 1980, could be said to belong to the so-called *shanghen, Weltschmerz* style which was popular with certain Chinese writers several years ago.

Zhang Lin

The Stranger

Six-year-old Panpan had her own views about families. Some children had fathers, but others had not. She belonged to the latter, for she had never seen her father, and her mother had never mentioned him. In this respect, she felt superior to other children. If they misbehaved, they would get smacked by their fathers, and then howl and wince in pain. It was different when Panpan misbehaved, because she did not have a father with a large pair of hands to slap her, and her mother loved her so much that she never dealt with her in that way. Her mother's hands were for doing the washing, not for beating. Therefore, she was rather spoilt.

One evening, Panpan was reading a picture book, while her mother was knitting a sweater. Panpan didn't like the sweater. It was grey and very big. It couldn't be for her. At that moment, the door opened and in came a man. He stood there staring blankly, as if he had come to the wrong door. Looking up at the man, Panpan felt her heart jump. Who was he? An old man, perhaps, for he had a beard. His face was pale, like a potato which had just been peeled. He was rather like the enemy in the picture book she had just read. Friends of her family usually knocked at the door first. How dare he barge in uninvited?

'Why didn't you knock at the door? That's rude . . .' Panpan stared at the stranger.

But he was like a piece of wood, saying nothing, only gazing at her. She scrutinized him again. He couldn't be a good man. It seemed he had never seen a child before. How could an adult stare at her like that? Wasn't she pretty? She turned to her mother to see what she was doing. Oddly, her mother stood there, open-mouthed, as if wanting to cry out, but unable to speak. Her eyes were fixed on the stranger and her hands were trembling. Suddenly she threw herself at the stranger, clasping him in her arms, her face pressed hard against his. The stranger even kissed her cheek. Her mother wept. Seeing this, Panpan was angry. In tears, her mother must have been hurt by his prickly beard. Panpan was very brave. She went over and tried to separate them, tugging at her mother and pushing away the man. Despite all her efforts, she didn't succeed and feeling exasperated she cried too.

The stranger released her mother, squatted down and looked at Panpan, saying, 'My, what a big girl!' Then he said to her mother, 'At that time, you were pregnant . . . I thought you had married again . . .'

'How can you say such a thing?' Her mother stopped him, 'I'd wait for you until death! I knew you weren't a reactionary! You weren't!' Her mother put her mouth to his ear and whispered softly in it. Then she embraced him again, holding him tightly, as if afraid he would disappear.

Panpan did not understand what they were whispering about and she started to hate her mother too. Her mother only embraced her in that way, never others. But Panpan certainly hated the stranger more. Her mother would never have behaved like that, if he hadn't appeared.

Letting her mother go, the man squatted down again, his face close to Panpan. 'What a pretty girl! Just like your mother!'

Looking at the strange pale face and beard, Panpan thought he had an ugly face! A smell of sweat overwhelmed her nostrils. Covering her nose, she stepped backwards. But the stranger held her hand and said, 'You can call me "Daddy". I'm your father!'

Now Panpan got angry. She pulled away her hand and said, 'I haven't got a daddy.'

Her mother squatted down and, putting her mouth to Panpan's ear, said very gently, 'But you *do* have a daddy. He's your daddy!'

Panpan glanced at the stranger again. How ugly and dirty he

was! Even if she wanted a daddy, she didn't want such an ugly one!

'You're not my daddy!' she screamed.

The room immediately became very quiet, as if her scream had frozen the world. Everything stopped.

A moment later, the man stood up, turned round and buried his face in his hands, his shoulders quivering. Her mother went over, put her hands on the man's shoulders and laid her head against his chest, saying in a soft and quavering voice, 'She's just a child! Don't mind her words . . . Please . . .'

The man shook his head and his shoulders heaved. Suddenly he started to cry. Her mother wanted to say something, but as she opened her mouth, she too began to sob. Seeing her mother in tears, Panpan felt sad. It was all the fault of that man. She wanted to tell him to leave. If her uncle were here, it would be much better. He would drive the man away. He was very strong.

Her mother turned round and came over to Panpan. She entreated in a low voice, 'Be a good girl, Panpan. Go and call him "Daddy"!'

Averting her eyes, stubborn Panpan said deliberately and loudly, 'He's *not* my daddy! I don't want a daddy!'

Even entreaties were useless. Her mother angrily gave Panpan a few slaps on her bottom and ordered in a severe voice, 'Go on! Call him "Daddy"!'

This was the first time her mother had beaten her. Panpan felt terribly hurt and wronged. Her mother was treating the man better than her! She cried bitterly, her feet kicking the floor, as if she was beating a drum. She shouted, 'Go away! You go away!'

The man said to her mother, 'I'll stay in the kitchen for a while. You put her to bed . . . After she's asleep, I'll come back.' So saying, he went to the kitchen. Her mother was a little tired. Leaning against the door, she wept, a handkerchief at her mouth.

Panpan understood the words this time. 'You'll come back again after I go to sleep. I won't sleep! I want to make you angry. I won't sleep!' she thought. She fastened the bolt of the kitchen door and then sat straight in the chair like an adult. With her eyes wide open, she tried not to blink. From the kitchen came the sound of the man sobbing.

'I won't sleep. I'll make you angry!' Panpan determined.

But she was only a child. After a moment, she started to yawn, closing her black lashes. In her sleep, she still insisted, 'I haven't got a daddy . . . I don't want a daddy!'

Translated by Wu Xiong

Wang Meng

Wang Meng is one of the most active of contemporary writers, although he too has endured the same vicissitudes that most intellectuals have had somehow to survive. He was born in Beijing in 1934, and unlike many of these writers, he has an intellectual background. His parents were intellectuals and as a student he was particularly bright and very much favoured by his teachers. He went into youth work after 1949, no doubt with the Communist Youth League. His first novel, *Eternal Youth*, written in 1953, reflects as its title suggests, his intimate knowledge of young people. This novel, with its emphasis on the youthful idealism of a group of secondary school students, attracted notice from people in the Chinese literary sphere. He then turned his attention to short story writing. *Winter Rain, Little Bean, The New Year Festival* and *The Young Newcomer to the Organization Department*, are among his most memorable stories. The latter, exploring as it did some of the organizational and bureaucratic fustiness of the Organization Department through the eyes of the enthusiastic new broom, was the trigger for a campaign of criticism that was instigated against him and led to his political disgrace in the anti-Rightist campaign of 1957. He was denounced, in the jargon of the time, as 'a rightist element who is anti-party and anti-socialism'. This ended his public career as a writer for almost twenty years. He spent the first five labouring on a farm in a village on the outskirts of Beijing. In 1964, as the political climate became harsher, he was relegated to distant Xinjiang, where working conditions were much more arduous than in the small rural village near Beijing, and the climate was much harsher. Here he lived in the typical mud house of the Uighur peasant and shared their agricultural life. His spirit was not daunted by his experience as is evident from a poem he wrote on arriving in Xinjiang. His scholarly background shows here since the poem is classical in form but modern in diction:

> *Through matters of life and death*
> *my blood does not run cold*
> *Through storm and turmoil my will*
> *remains firm*
> *With the light of spring I will*
> *sing without regret*
> *I have only my poor self to give to*
> *this cold border post.*

He put his time amongst the Uighurs to good use by learning their language. He also had access to books and read extensively in foreign literature. This has been of great benefit to his subsequent work as a writer and translator. Since his rehabilitation in 1976 he was written six novellas, works considered by the critics to outstrip his earlier stories both in terms of their literary craftsmanship and the depth and scope of his treatment of subject. Some critics considered that these recent stories have been affected by the stream of consciousness technique of writing. He scorns this suggestion:

> If people are going to dismiss my work as merely stream of consciousness, then such superficial criticism simply makes me feel sad.

A Spate of Visitors was published in the *People's Daily* on 12 January 1980.

Wang Meng
A Spate of Visitors

Who was he?

He was so keen on efficiency and saving time that after going to the liberated area he changed his name to Ding Yi. However, during the Cultural Revolution he, too, came under fire.

There was nothing special about his appearance or voice, and he wore his cadre's blue gabardine jacket all the year round. So some people were afraid that even his wife would find it hard to spot him in the crowd of customers in a department store. Fortunately he had two minor characteristics—it seems no one can be quite free from distinctive features. One was the bulge at the back of his head, the other his frequent frown. His critics had attributed the bulge to 'a reactionary skull', the frown to his negative outlook.

He was bull-headed. In the countryside it was the unwritten rule to keep separate accounts. That for the beginning of the year contained a plan, quota, guarantee and grandiose statements; that for the end recorded the yield, the amount of grain stored and sold to the state and the value of output. The two accounts were never compared or checked to see if they tallied. But this was not Ding Yi's way. He insisted on comparing them and investigating any discrepancies. It wouldn't have mattered if he had just ticked off the cadres in the production brigade and commune, but he took the accounts with him to the Party committees in the county and prefecture to protest. This happened in 1959. All of a sudden the situation grew tense as everyone there woke up to a sharpening in the acute, complex class struggle. Not only was he denounced and labelled a 'Rightist', but all the ex-landlords, rich peasants, their children and grandchildren as well as those Rightists who had been sent from the provincial capital to do physical labour in the countryside were reinvestigated and forced to make a clean breast of their relations with him.

Ding Yi's position went from bad to worse.

However, a settlement always comes in the end. In January 1979, Ding Yi was rehabilitated, and in June that year, thirty years after he joined the revolution, when he was more than fifty, he regained his Party membership and was appointed director of the county's Rose-fragrance Paste Factory.

Many people congratulated him, but he frowned and asked 'What for?' Others told him they thought he deserved a higher position; but without hearing them out he turned away. Yet others said that he had grown cocky again, having never really tucked his tail between his legs.

He made his rounds in the small factory day and night, his jacket often smeared with paste which smelt quite unlike the scent of roses. When his wife called him a poor wretch he only smiled.

So, he had very few visitors.

Ding Yi stirs up a hornet's nest

At his new post Ding Yi discovered two big problems. Here, the word 'discover' is hardly appropriate, because these two problems were as obvious as lice on a bald head. They made him frown and rack his brains every day. First, there was no proper control of the by-product of paste, gluten, which the workers divided among themselves to sell, give to friends or exchange for other goods. This was scandalous. Secondly, the labour discipline was so lax that the foreman sometimes tripped over people sound asleep during their work shifts. So, after consulting everyone concerned, Ding Yi drew up a set of regulations and a system of rewards and penalties. In fact, these were nothing new, just standard practice.

A month went by. In May, Ding Yi decided to make an example of a contract worker named Gong Ding. For one thing, this young man had stayed away from work for four months without asking for leave. For another, he came bold as brass to the factory to demand gluten, and if given none cursed or beat the man in charge. Furthermore, he turned a deaf ear to reprimands. So Ding Yi asked the Party branch committee, Youth League committee, trade union, personnel office and all the other departments to discuss Gong Ding's case. Though he prodded them three times a day, it took them a month and a half to agree to his proposal that this recalcitrant worker should be dismissed. On June 21, an announcement was put up in the factory: In accordance with regulations, Gong Ding's contract was terminated.

Some people knew that Gong Ding was a distant relative of the first county Party secretary, Li, and felt it was a mistake to fire him, but they did not like to say so. After all, he was only a distant relative. So, the decision was finally reached and announced.

Psychological warfare breaks out

Three hours after the announcment was put up, Ding Yi began to have callers. The first was Old Liu from the county Party committee office. Fifty-seven years old, with an affable expression, he prided himself on his diplomacy and good relations on all sides. Smilingly, he put one hand on Ding Yi's shoulder. 'Listen to me, Old Ding,' he said. 'You've worked hard and run the factory well. But as for Gong Ding's case . . .' Lowering his voice he explained Gong's relationship to the first county Party secretary. He added, 'Of course, this has no bearing on his case. You're right to take disciplinary action. Secretary Li would be grateful to you if he knew. It's you I'm thinking of. You'd better not fire him. He'll still have to stay in China, in our county, if he's kicked out. We'll still be responsible for him, and he's bound to ask Secretary Li for help. So, better let him off with a warning.' He reasoned so earnestly and patiently that Ding Yi began to waver. Just then, however, Zhou, head of the county industrial bureau, rang up.

'What's come over you?' he bellowed. 'Why pick a relative of the county Party secretary to make an example of? What are people going to think? Hurry up and revoke your decision!'

'No, the decision stands!' replied Ding Yi loudly as he hung up the receiver. His face grim, he turned to Old Liu and said, 'Outrageous!'

However, visitors kept coming. At dusk, Old Zhao, chairman of the county revolutionary committee, arrived. Zhao had worked in the county since land reform. He was most influential and strongly entrenched. With a certain reserve he shook hands languidly with Ding Yi, then paced the room while issuing his instructions, not even glancing at Ding.

'We must be prudent, mustn't oversimplify issues. Nowadays people are very sensitive. Gong Ding's dismissal would cause general dismay. In view of this, it's more judicious not to fire him.'

He said no more, thinking this directive sufficient. He had paced the room slowly enunciating each word, as if weighing and savouring it. Yes, to him his words were as tasty as spiced beef.

When Ding Yi went home after dark, his wife put in her twopence worth as well. Of course, she scolded him out of wifely concern.

'You perishing old fool! Don't you see what you've gone and done? Has messing about with paste all day made you soft-headed? You stick to principles? Why aren't you a member of the politburo? Remember the bashing you got in 1966? Your principles not only got you into trouble but me and the children too.'

This outburst stemmed from bitter resentment and love. And the tears she shed were more eloquent than words. Ding Yi sighed, and was just about to reason with her when in came another visitor. It was Young Xiao, who had befriended Ding Yi when he was in disgrace. Young Xiao had studied in the Philosophy Department of Beijing University where he was labelled a Rightist. Later he had managed to get a job in the county's electricity company. Recently, after his name was cleared, he had been promoted to be a buyer. He was short, big-nosed and extremely ugly. But the more pressure put on him, the more cheery, quick-witted and engaging he grew. His motto was: If someone slaps your face, turn the other cheek. He reckoned that this tactic succeeded three times out of four.

Young Xiao's arrival filled the house with laughter. The first thing he did after taking a seat was to finish up the dumplings left by Ding Yi and his wife who had lost their appetite. Then he asked after everyone in the family, saying admiringly, 'How lucky you are to have so many relatives.' Next he told them that he would soon buy and send over the TV set, a real bargain, they had long wanted. Finally he related various funny stories about their county, China and other countries till the whole family was roaring with laughter.

Why aren't you a cross-talk actor?' Ding Yi asked.

'I don't want to do Hou Baolin* out of a job. He's my uncle on my mother's side, you know.'

There was another roar of laughter.

Young Xiao took advantage of this to launch his offensive. 'Why, there's a small matter I nearly forgot,' he said. 'It's about that young rascal Gong. He's a real shit! I'll dress him down next time I see him. But Old Ding, you mustn't go too far. You and I haven't got much footing here. Nor do we have powerful backing or commodities that other people want. We depend entirely on keeping in with others. Big shots rely on their power, we nobodies on our connections. With power they can get anything they want; by keeping on good terms with others we can make do. So don't be so bull-headed. If you haven't learned anything else all these years, you should have learned how to veer. . . I know, you needn't explain it to me. The decision has been announced; still, it can be changed. Even the Constitution can be changed, and Chairman Mao made revisions in his writings. You're only a small factory director. Think you're more infallible than Chairman Mao and the Constitution? Go on! Get Gong Ding back. I must make myself clear. It's not the county secretary who sent me here, I came on my own initiative, having your interests at heart. Of course, Gong Ding did ask me to come and I told him, "Don't you worry. Old Ding will do me a little favour like this."'

* One of China's most popular comedians.

He certainly had the gift of the gab, able to range from the sublime to the vulgar, to crack jokes or to scoff.

Originally, Ding Yi had not known that Gong Ding was a distant relative of the county's first secretary, and he was not unwilling to reconsider the case. But all these visitors put him on his guard. If it hadn't been the first secretary's relative, would so many people have come to urge him to 'be prudent', 'not to oversimplify issues' and to 'consider the consequences'? This question preoccupied him, to the exclusion of considerations.

In his annoyance he sent Young Xiao packing.

Two days passed. June 23, Sunday, was a hot, long, midsummer day. Mosquitoes had kept Ding awake the previous night, and he had no appetite. At half past four that morning, a visitor arrived by bus. He was Ding Yi's brother-in-law. Tall, bespectacled and bald, he had studied in the Marxist-Leninist Institute in the 1950s and was now teaching in the prefectural Party school. He was the best known theorist in the prefecture and enjoyed great prestige. When listening to his lectures, grassroots cadres kept nodding their heads just like chickens pecking millet from the ground. He was the seventeenth visitor in the past two days. As soon as he set foot in the room, he began to talk from a theoretical point of view.

'Socialist society is a transition period in which there exist the scars of capitalism and pre-capitalism. They are inevitable and independent of man's will. This society is superior but not yet mature or perfect. It's only a transition. . .' After this abstract preamble, he continued:

'So we say, leaders' power, their likes and dislikes, their impressions, are of vital importance. They cannot be overlooked and very often play the decisive role. We are realists, not utopian socialists like Owen and Fourier.' (Ding Yi thought: Am I a utopian socialist? This label doesn't sound too bad.) 'We are not children or pedants. Our socialism is built on the ground under our feet, which, though beautiful, is rather backward and undeveloped.' (Ding Yi thought: Have I ever wanted to fly to paradise?) 'So when we do any work, we must take all factors into consideration. To use an algebraic formula, there are ''N'' factors, not one. The more complicated the world is, the larger the ''N''. . . So, brother, you were too hasty in handling Gong Ding's case. You didn't use your brain.' (Ding Yi thought: A fine brain *you* have, holding forth like this!) 'Don't make a gross error, brother. Be statesmanlike. Cancel your decision and invite Gong Ding back.'

Ding Yi's wife hastily put in, 'That's right, that's right!' A pleased smile appeared on her face. It dawned on Ding Yi that she had asked her theorist brother to talk him round.

While listening, Ding Yi had felt as if his chest was stuffed with hog bristles. His face looked as if he was swallowing a worm. After he had listened attentively for forty minutes, he simply asked, 'Did you teach these theories in your Party school?'

Within the twenty-one hours from the arrival of the theorist till 1.45 the next morning, visitors kept coming and going. Some let loose a flood of eloquence, as if they could bring the dying back to life. Some blustered as if they would swallow up the whole world. Some bowed and scraped like swinging willow branches. Some had a well-thought-out plan which they enunciated a word or two at a time, determined not to desist till their goal was reached or, failing that, to hurl Ding Yi over a cliff rather than leave his family in peace. Some brought with them presents ranging from flowers to rancid bean curd. Some promised him a flat with a southern exposure or a brand-new bicycle. Some warned him that he was isolating himself and would come to no good end. Some spoke of the need to protect the Party's prestige—to save the first secretary's face. Some worried about his safety and the fate of his family, some about preserving unity in the country, yet others about human rights, democracy and freedom.

These visitors included Ding Yi's old colleagues, schoolmates, superiors, subordinates, comrades-in-arms, fellow patients in hospital, fellow sufferers, 'wine-and-meat' friends and the descendants of his late friends. Some of them were aged people with high prestige, others were promising young ones. Even those who had been in favour of his decision in the factory came over to state that they had changed their minds.

Although their motives and manner of speaking differed, they agreed on one point: Gong Ding must not be fired.

Ding Yi had never thought he knew so many people and was known to so many. He could not understand their keen concern for Gong Ding or why his disciplinary action against a contract worker, a hooligan and a distant relative of the county secretary had stirred up such a hornet's nest. He was fast becoming a public enemy! He could neither eat nor rest, nor do any chores. His Sunday was spoilt. He wanted to scream, to smash things, to beat someone up. But instead he gritted his teeth and listened impassively warning himself, 'Keep cool and you'll win through!'

Among the visitors was a star whom Ding Yi had admired when young. Forty years ago, she had been the best known actress in the province. And Ding Yi in his teens was infatuated for a spell with this woman thirteen years older than himself, although they did not know each other. He had never told anyone of his romantic dream. It was only in the Cultural Revolution when he was undergoing 'labour reform' that he had the luck to meet her, an old lady who had retired and now weighed more than eighty kilograms. Due to his oriental, old-fashioned devotion, Ding Yi had always had a special affection for her. To his surprise this 'queen' of earlier times also arrived by a donkey cart that day. Sitting on the bed, she prattled through the gaps in her teeth:

'I should have come to see you earlier, Young Ding. Look at me, aren't I an old witch? I don't know why I've aged so suddenly. Why do so many things come to an end before they've really started? It's like the stage: you're still making up when the music for the final curtain sounds. . .'

Her lamentation over the transience of life made Ding Yi's eyes moist with tears. Of all his visitors that day she seemed to him the only one who had called on him out of pure friendship. But what she went on to say took him aback:

'I hear you're a real martinet. That's no way to run a factory. It turns people against you, doesn't it? Do unto others as you would be done by. Haven't you learned anything from your own experience? You'd better not be too hard on young people.'

Still, Ding Yi was grateful to her, recalling his youthful dreams. Among the visitors that day, she was the only one who made no mention of Rose-fragrance Paste Factory, Gong Ding and the county secretary.

Some statistics

I hope readers will excuse me if now I depart from the normal narrative style to publish some correct but well-nigh unbelievable statistics.

In the 12 days from 21 June to 2 July, the visitors who came to plead for Gong Ding totalled 199.5 (the former actress didn't mention his name but had him in mind, so she is counted in as 0.5). 33 people telephoned. 27 wrote letters. 53 or 27% really showed keen concern for Ding Yi and were afraid he would run into trouble. 20 or 10% were sent by Gong Ding; 1 or 0.5% by Secretary Li. 63 or 32% were sent by people approached directly or indirectly by Secretary Li. 8 or 4% were asked by Ding Yi's wife to talk round her 'die-hard' husband. 46 or 23% were not sent by anyone and did not know Ding Yi but came on their own initiative to do Secretary Li a service. The remaining 4% came for no clear reasons.

Ding Yi refused all his visitors' requests. His stubbornness enraged 85% of them, who immediately spread word that he was a fool. Ding Yi's petty appointment had gone to his head, they claimed, making him stubborn and unreasonable, and cutting him off from the masses. They asserted that he was fishing for fame and credit, that he had ulterior motives and was taking this chance to vent his spite because the county Party committee had not promoted him to a higher position. Some said he was crazy and had always been reactionary, that he should never have been rehabilitated. Assuming that each of them spoke to at least ten people, 1,700 heard talk of this kind. For a while public opinion was strongly against him. It seemed all were out for his blood. His wife fell ill and her life was only saved by emergency measures. Even the nurse in charge of the oxygen cylinder took the chance to ask Ding Yi to change his mind.

Incidents of this kind happen quickly and end quickly too. They are like the breakfast queues in restaurants, which form as soon as fried cakes and porridge are served and disperse immediately after the food is sold out, no matter how angry those who missed out on the fried cakes are. By August there was no further talk of the case, and by September it had escaped people's minds. Meanwhile, the production in the paste factory had gone up each day. By October, great changes had taken place. When talking together, people stuck up their thumbs saying, 'Old Ding Yi really knows a thing or two!'

By December, the fame of the paste factory really had the fragrance of roses. It had became a model for all the small enterprises in the province. The Rose-fragrance Paste it produced was consistently of first-rate quality. Ding Yi went to attend a meeting in the provincial capital at which he was asked to report his experience. He went on to the rostrum, his face flushed, and said, 'Communists are made of steel, not paste . . .'

This caused a general sensation.

He added, 'If we don't get down to business, our country's done for!'

He broke off there, choking, and tears ran down his cheeks.

There was a solemn silence for a moment in the auditorium.

Then, thunderous applause!

Translated by Xiong Zhenru

Malqinhu

He is the most notable of the first generation of Mongolian writers. Born in Inner Mongolia in 1930, he attended a Mongolian language secondary school. His preparation for literary work involved a period in the Inner Mongolia Literary Workers' Troup, to which he was transferred after a stint as a cavalry man in the Eighth Route Army, which he had joined in 1945. He is said to have read avidly all he could get his hands on. His first story, *People of the Kolqin Prairies,* was the account of an actual incident the discovery, pursuit and capture of an escaped criminal by a young Mongolian girl. This caught the attention of people in the literary world and he was transferred to Beijing, where he was given the opportunity to develop his potential further at the Institute for Literary Instruction, which is run by the Chinese Writers' Association. Malqinhu is now a member of the Executive of the Association. His works include two volumes of short stories—*The Rites of Spring* (1954) and *The Colourful Prairies* (1962); a novel in two parts— *Vast Prairies* (Part One completed in 1956 and Part Two after 1979); the novella *The First Days of Summer* and the screenplays *The Desert in Spring* and *Homeland, Our Mother*. These last have all been written since 1979. *The Story of the Living Buddha* was published in the *People's Daily* on 12 February 1980.

Malqinhu

The Story of a Living Buddha

My home was a village named Bayinhot, the seat of our Banner[1] Prince. In this village I passed my 'golden childhood', now shrouded in a somewhat dim and mysterious light which evokes a deep nostalgia in me.

Our neighbour was a lama named Tegus. According to tradition, lamas should not marry. However, Tegus was not only married, but even had a family. I still have not managed to understand how this could have come about.

Lama Tegus had three sons. The eldest was called Hasenjiab, the second Garhe and the third Malaha. Malaha was the same age as I. When we were only beginning to learn to speak, the two of us, bottoms bare, played together on the sand dumps in front of our houses. By the time we were old enough to wear open-seat pants, we had already become fast friends.

Little Malaha was a very handsome boy. He had fine eyebrows and clear eyes, red lips, white teeth, a round face, a high nose and a full head of jet-black curly hair. His only poor feature were his ears, which were too long. But our elders said that this was a 'feature of Buddha', and that persons who had such long dangling ears were destined to have good fortune. I am not too sure exactly what is meant by good fortune. But anyhow Malaha was then much wiser, abler and bolder than I. I admired him very much.

My family was extremely poor. His was a little better off. In the spring of the year when I was about six years old, our village was afflicted with famine. With the exception of the

1. An administrative district at county level in the Inner Mongolia Autonomous Region.

Banner Prince and a few households of Bayan[2], the families in
our village had nothing to eat. One evening little Malaha came
to me and said, 'Get your basket, let's go and climb the elm
trees and collect elm-pods!'

'Where shall we go on a dark night like this?'

'That large pasture in front of the Banner Prince's mansion,
where we can climb up those big elms.'

I was frightened on hearing this, and said quickly, 'They are
holy trees. Haven't you seen people go there every year to
kowtow to them? Who'd dare climb up them? The Prince
would cut off our legs if he knew.'

Malaha waved his hand and said, '*Hai*! Holy trees, what's
that? Who's ever seen a holy spirit? Have you seen one?'

I shook my small bald head.

'Let's go then before the moon comes up. Hurry up! We'll
climb the trees and get the pods!'

Elm-pods, when mixed with flour chaff and steamed, were
good to eat. Especially in famine years, they were a rare relish
for the poor. Knowing that we had nothing to cook tomorrow, I
summoned up my courage, took my basket and followed him
to the large pasture in front of the Banner Prince's mansion.

Little Malaha was a real devil. He saw not far from us an old
spotted cow grazing with her neck stretched out. Telling me to
do as he did, he lay down on the grass and crept slowly like a
frog towards the cow. At first, I didn't know what was in his
mind. Then I saw him drive the cow before him with a branch,
to shield us so that we could proceed behind her towards a holy
tree. I then realized that this would prevent the sentries in the
fort of the Banner Prince's mansion from discovering us. The
old spotted cow was quite obedient. Covering us with her huge
body, she led us to a large holy tree and then swaying her long
tail moved aside to graze.

The dark night made the large holy tree appear pitch black,
swaying to and fro in a way that struck terror into me. While I
was standing there dumbly, little Malaha had already nimbly
climbed up the tree. I climbed up after him. It was truly a holy

2. The Mongolian word for 'rich man'.

tree, still flourishing despite the dry season. Soon we had gathered two large basketfuls of elm-pods. A big, red moon had risen in the eastern sky, seeming so tender, mysterious and affectionate. Malaha and I were both fascinated by the bewitching and majestic sight of the moon rising. We carefully hung our baskets full of elm-pods on a branch, and waved our hands happily at the smiling moon from our stations high up the holy tree . . .

The moon rose higher, casting its silvery light all over the pasture. I suddenly thought about our return home and asked Malaha anxiously, 'The moon's so bright, how can we escape from the pasture?'

'We must ask the old cow to help us again,' he said.

When we had got away from the pasture, we put the two baskets of elm-pods on the ground and rolled about in high glee. We are quite tired after the tension of the escape and the joyous play that followed. We lay down with outstretched limbs on the dew-soaked meadow and gazed silently at the deep blue night sky. Our limited powers of imagination now had free play. What is the sky made of? Why is it such a deep blue? Is there another world behind the deep blue sky, and are there virtuous and cultivated persons residing there, as the old Buddhists said? There certainly wouldn't be a fierce Banner Prince, nor wretched poor people, and what's more, there wouldn't be any need to live on elm-pods . .

The following day, both our households had a sweet-smelling meal of steamed elm-pods mixed with flour chaff.

That year we had a dry spring and a water-logged summer. Rain fell continuously from early summer, and the stream in our neighbourhood rose high enough for people to catch small fish in it. One day, little Malaha came running to find me, his brow beaded with sweat.

'Let's go and catch fish in the stream,' he said. 'It's nice and cool.'

I was feeling unbearably bored at home, so I went with him without a murmur.

The flooding had ended. The water in the stream was so clear that one could see down to the bottom. At first sight, the multicoloured pebbles in the stream appeared like so many leaping small fish. We stripped off our clothes and plunged in. A pleasant feeling of coolness spread rapidly all over my body, and even penetrated into my heart. We stood stark naked in the stream, splashing water on each other and frolicking about, forgetting our original object of catching fish.

The next day, around noon, what was to me an almost unthinkable piece of news circulated through the village. Little Malaha, who just yesterday was my bare-bottomed fishing companion, had been chosen by the Gegen Monastery as a Living Buddha! To say that he was chosen as a Living Buddha is not quite correct. According to Buddhist teaching, a Living Buddha is a reincarnation of another in a previous life. This is to say, the Living Buddha in his previous life writes down in liquid gold on red satin where and in which family he will be born again, puts it in a sealed engraved silver pot and keeps it in a certain secret place. After the death of the Living Buddha, a conference of senior lamas, presided over by his erstwhile 'sutra teacher', is held, the silver pot is unsealed in public and the testament is read out to the meeting. Then, in accordance with the directions given in the occult and riddle-like posthumous script, a search for the reincarnated Living Buddha is made.

It was reported that the previous Living Buddha of the Gegen Monastery had written that the characteristics of the family he was to be born into were as follows: First, the first syllables of the names of the three sons were in the order of the Mongolian alphabet—A, Na, Ba, Ha, Ga, Ma . . . ; thus if the first syllable of the name of his eldest brother was 'Ha', that of the second brother would be 'Ga' and that of himself 'Ma'. Secondly, eight hundred and ten steps to the southeast of their house was a large tree which could not be encircled by five persons with their hands joined together. And thirdly, eight hundred and ten steps to the northwest of their house and three feet underground was a lump of granite as big as an ox head. It was not enough to find a family with three sons whose names began with the syllables Ha, Ga and Ma, but the family's home must conform to the two other circumstances described.

Only then could the lamas declare that the new Living Buddha's family had been found.

The envoys sent out by the Gegen Monastery took several years to make secret investigations and inquiries according to the directions given, and finally concluded that my little companion Malaha was the new Living Buddha they were looking for. Thus little Malaha who had been catching fish in the river with me yesterday changed overnight from a boy into a deity—the eighth Living Buddha of the Gegen Monastery.

This was a momentous event. All the Buddhists in the village seemed to share some of the glory. Every one of them was smiling and the whole village was bubbling over like a cauldron of boiling water. At noon, the Leading Senior Lama of the Gegen Monastery announced that, from two o'clock that afternoon, Living Buddha Malaha would receive the worship of the villagers.

My mother was a devout Buddhist. She told me to wash my hands and face and get ready to go at the appointed time to pay homage to Living Buddha Malaha. Hearing this, I couldn't help laughing aloud. Seeing me act in such a sacrilegious manner, she gave my ear a sharp tug and sternly bade me, 'Don't laugh!' I dared not laugh again.

Soon it was two o'clock, and Mother took me to kowtow to Malaha. My childish curiosity made me want to find out what my little companion who had become a Living Buddha now looked like.

I followed my mother to the gate of Malaha's home. A large number of men, women and children had already gathered there. As Malaha was now a Living Buddha, the distinction of generations in the outside world did not apply to him any more. Those he called uncles and aunts or even granddads and grandmas yesterday had also to come and pay homage to him and receive his benediction today. When after some time it was our turn to go inside and kowtow to the Living Buddha, my heart began to beat fast, for I was afraid. I was pushed indoors.

I saw Malaha sitting upright in the centre of the *kang*[3], with a

3. A heatable brick bed.

borrowed redwood *kang* table in front of him, upon which was placed a volume of Buddhist sutras and a silver pot containing 'holy water' with a peacock feather stuck in it. This peacock feather was used to spray 'holy water' on worshippers. When I entered, little Malaha at once smiled at me. I don't know whether I myself smiled or not. On either side of Malaha sat his mother and his 'sutra teacher'. The old sutra teacher's eyelids and lips were loose and pendulous, and there were two deep furrows on each side of his mouth. His face was gloomy and he looked quite frightening. I dared not keep looking at him. My mother had already knelt down on the ground, putting her palms together devoutly and kowtowing three times. I hastened to imitate her and kowtow to Malaha. When I had kowtowed the first time and lifted my head to look at him, our eyes met. He smiled his usual innocent smile, waved his hand and made a face at me. I dared not smile, but he was so pleased with himself that he laughed outright. The sutra teacher was evidently much offended at such behaviour, and made two loud sniffs in warning. Malaha's mother became alarmed and hastened to caution him in a kind but stern tone, 'Living Buddha, sit quietly and don't be naughty!'

When my mother and I had finished our worship, Malaha took up the sutra volume, of which he didn't know a word, and with it touched our foreheads lightly. He then sprayed some drops of 'holy water' on our heads with the peacock plume. The ritual was concluded. When Mother was taking me out of the house, I boldly looked back once again at little Malaha to take leave of him. My little companion raised his eyebrows and knowingly winked at me as if to say: You just wait; we'll go and climb the tree again to gather elm-pods, and to catch fish in the stream.

I could not help thinking: Malaha had not been changed into a Buddha, he was still my little companion.

At four o'clock the next morning, Living Buddha Malaha was to set out on his trip to take his place in the monastery. All our villagers went very early to the sides of the earthen road which was sprinkled with water, to wait there and see him off. I woke up at dawn that day, and the thought that I would soon have to part with my little companion made me extremely sad. I wanted to cry when standing among the crowd outside the village. But the atmosphere was so solemn and quiet that I did not dare. I just stared at the entrance of the village where Malaha was to appear.

Soon there came the boisterous sounds of a lama band, which consisted of gold and silver bugles, ram-horn trumpets, a big bass trumpet more than ten feet long and borne by two small lamas, eight drums and ten pairs of cymbals. There was nothing musical about the fearful, ear-splitting din produced. In this great hubbub, a large golden yellow object moved towards us, coming nearer and nearer. The people kneeling waiting on the sides of the road began to kowtow incessantly as the golden yellow object approached. The Living Buddha Malaha's train was now before us. Hoping for a final look at my little companion, I knelt there dumbly, forgetting to pay my respects. 'Kowtow, kowtow!' Mother urged. In confusion I bent over once, and then lifted my head again to look at Malaha. Ha! I saw a train of nine big tall horses each covered with a large yellow satin cloth, reaching almost to the ground. Apart from the lamas who were acting as grooms, the priests and members of Malaha's family followed behind the nine horses. Malaha, dressed in a yellow robe, looking lonely and pathetic, rode on the fifth horse. Although there were four lamas looking after him on both sides, he was still very much afraid of being thrown, and was gingerly clinging to the reins. When he came before me, he looked over our bent heads. He seemed to have seen me, and again, not to have seen me. His thick eyebrows were closely knitted and his face was full of the pain and sorrow of parting from his native place, his relatives and companions. It seemed to me that there were tears in the corners of his eyes.

The golden yellow object gradually moved away and was lost in the yellow dust. The villagers got up one after another, their foreheads all stained with earth. Those who had kowtowed more often had more earth on their foreheads. These people were so deeply immersed in religious devotion that they forgot to wipe their foreheads with their cuffs.

When I followed the crowd back to the village, I felt as if robbed of something, or as if two young oxen were fighting inside my heart. It was unbearable! I did not eat or drink that whole day. I went alone to sit silently with fixed eyes in the shade of the trees on the large pasture ground. When it had grown very late Mother found me and took me home.

Three years elapsed, and I entered a western-style school.

One day when I returned home from school, I found my mother's poverty-wrinkled face bright with happiness. 'Living Buddha Malaha will come home tomorrow to receive the worship of his fellow villagers,' she told me. In my mind filled with the letters of the Mongolian alphabet there appeared once more the image of my beloved little companion Malaha.

Living Buddha Malaha was to receive the worship of his fellow villagers on the top of the high white marble steps before the main hall of an ancient lamasery in the eastern part of the village. It was said that to kowtow to a Living Buddha could dispel misfortune and turn disaster into good luck. Consequently, some old people, hoping to atone for the 'sins' they had committed in their present lifetime and to enjoy 'peace and happiness' in their next life, would prostrate themselves and kowtow at every step right from their doorway until they came before the feet of the Living Buddha. In order to do so, some even got up at midnight. Having been a pupil in a western-style school for several years, I was already quite indifferent to religion. I was not interested in looking at the magnificent structure of the monastery, or in the solemnity of the ceremony, but concentrated on elbowing my way through the crowd to a place near the Living Buddha to take a careful look at my childhood companion, to find out what, after all, he was like now. Amidst the dense smoke of incense-sticks I was carried by the stream of people before little Malaha — no, Living Buddha Malaha. He was sitting on a thick yellow satin cushion at the top of the steps, while I was kneeling beneath at the bottom of the steps on a hard flagstone. I raised my head, opened my eyes wide and stared. I quickly discovered that my little companion Malaha had completely changed. His cheeks were emaciated, his eye-sockets deeply sunken and his face was ashy white, devoid of expression. His eyes especially appeared weary and lack-lustre. He seemed to have recognized me, and rolled his eyes once. But without waiting for my reaction, he immediately resumed his 'Buddha appearance'; his eyes were again motionless. Alas! Only three years and my little companion had changed from an innocent lively child into such a cold and apathetic 'god'. I felt cut to the heart.

In the summer when Malaha had been a Living Buddha for a full five years, a grand gathering was held by the Gegen Monastery, during which Living Buddha Malaha would expound Buddhist sutras. I went with our neighbours to witness this magnificent occasion. On the last day, the Leading Senior Lama of the Gegen Monastery declared: Living Buddha Malaha would receive the worship of the laity that evening.

In the evening, the monastery was filled with a large crowd of worshippers. I stood at the end of a long stream of hurrying people, and looked from a distance of about a hundred metres at the Living Buddha's throne. I saw several ever-burning lamps in the lofty main hall. Although every bronze oil cup of each lamp could contain fifty catties of butter, the light was still not strong enough for me to see his face clearly. All I could see was a figure draped in a yellow cloak, with a yellow satin hood on his head, his palms together, sitting there motionless like an earthen idol in a large monastery.

I made a detour from the back of the main hall to the front of the Living Buddha. All the devout Buddhists there were in a frenzy, unable to restrain their emotion. Some were praying loudly, others begging tearfully for his blessing. They were bowing low, ready to kneel down at any moment. The Living Buddha Malaha, however, with his eyes closed, took no notice of his devout, fanatical worshippers; he did not even deign to move an eyelash. To attract his attention I deliberately straightened up and walked right up to him, hoping that he would turn his eyes to look at me again. But my hopes were disappointed. Suddenly I was emboldened, I don't know how, to call softly several times to the living idol draped with yellow satin, 'Malaha, it's me! Hello, it's me, Malaha!' Although my cry was not loud, I was sure he could hear me. But he made not the slightest response. My heart sank like a stone: Was it possible that he had really become a Buddha? In these overpowering and mysterious religious surroundings, I went down involuntarily on my knees before him and kowtowed several times in succession. When I got up again and dragged myself out of the monastery, I was heart-broken, crying loudly at the thought of having lost my dear childhood companion forever.

Several more decades passed. And now our people were masters of the new society.

Nurtured on the people's milk, I had grown from a poor, illiterate boy into a writer. I frequently recollected my own 'golden childhood', the months and years of struggle, and the many childhood companions and comrades-in-arms of my youth, who had become models for the characters that appeared in my writings, but for some reason I had failed to include little Malaha. Perhaps it was because he was no longer a man in my memory, but had become a Buddha. In my literary works, which depicted real life, what I required were men of flesh and blood, men of feeling, not earthen idols who could not even turn their eyes or react when their own names were called.

Rat-tat-tat!

I was sitting in my study and writing one quiet winter night when I heard someone knocking at the door. My mother who was eighty-six years old but still healthy, answered, 'Coming, coming,' and went to open the door. Then I suddenly heard my younger daughter crying, 'Papa, come here quick, Grandma has fainted!' I dropped my pen and hurried out. My old mother had not fainted, she was kowtowing repeatedly. Because my daughter had never seen this done before, she thought that her grandmother had fainted. Meanwhile, the guest had taken a stride forward and was carefully helping my mother up, saying, 'Aunty, you shouldn't do that now, I am a man, an ordinary man, not a Buddha!'

I turned to look at the visitor. He was neatly dressed. His temples were grey, the corners of his mouth drooped, and the hair on his balding head was brushed tidily backwards. He turned dirctly towards me after helping my mother up. Then, from his smiling eyes I recognized him: it was Malaha—my little childhood friend!

'Where have you been all these years?' I asked him after inviting him to my study and exchanging some words of greeting.

'I was travelling around practising medicine, staying wherever I could; but you mustn't think I was an itinerant quack peddling dogskin plasters.' He drank a mouthful of the tea I offered him and spoke calmly, with a note of self-mockery. 'As soon as our area was liberated, I turned over the affairs of the monastery to the Leading Senior Lama and began to study Mongolian and Tibetan medicine in the temple where I lived. The Mongolian and Tibetan people have a rich store of traditional medical knowledge.' So saying he took out an elaborately bound book from his bag. 'Here's the result of my forty years' research. It was published recently,' he told me.

I took the book from his hand and saw embossed on its cover the title, *Mongolian and Tibetan Pharmacopoeia*, in big golden characters in the Mongolian, Tibetan and Chinese languages. Underneath was printed the name of the author: 'Malaha'.

'In the nineteenth century these parts produced the well-known writer and historian Yinzhannaxi, and now in the twentieth century we have our celebrated doctor Malaha. This is something our people can be proud of!' I said elatedly.

Malaha's face was now quite mobile and it was clear that he felt deeply honoured. His intelligent eyes glowed.

'I've just attended a national conference on medical science in Shanghai, and came especially to see you on my way back.'

Malaha stayed with us for three days. On the eve of his departure I prepared some dishes and wine to bid him farewell. He was not a good drinker, but that evening he finished three cups in a row. The wine warmed our faces. The affection we had felt for each other as children came back to us again. We were both very happy. Thanks probably to the wine I had drunk, I blurted out a question which I had not yet had the courage to ask:

'Are you now Doctor Malaha, or Living Buddha Malaha? A

doctor is a man. But if you are still a Living Buddha, then you are not a man but a deity.'

Malaha sat in a reclining chair, a cup of tea in his hand. He smiled sadly, and said in a voice neither hurried nor slow:

'Ah! Of course, there are no deities in this world. But then, out of foolishness and to find something in which they can place their hopes, men create gods for themselves. A man worshipped as a god by his fellow-creatures has at first only a vague sense of being one. As time goes by he becomes convinced that he is one, and therefore acts like a god. Men then worship him more devoutly and believe in him more fanatically. They don't know that they have been made fools of. Creating a god is also making a fool of the man thus converted. And the man converted into a god then assumes the manner of a god to make fools of the people who have deified him. We have passed many thousands of years in this comedy of mutual trickery. These years have been a time of absurdity. But history ultimately will be written by the people themselves and these years of absurdity have already passed.'

Written on June 10, 1980, in Beijing.

Translated by Hu Zhihui

Bai Honghu and Yang Zhao

Hansuai, the Living Ghost, is one of a number of recent stories written by this husband and wife team. Both have literary backgrounds, having worked as editors of the journal *Literature of the Border Regions*. The wife, Bai Honghu, was born in 1921 in Yunnan. Yunnan is a multi-racial region where as many as twenty minority ethnic peoples co-exist with the Han Chinese. Her husband, Yang Zhao, is from Jiangxi, another western province. He was born there in 1928, but has lived in Yunnan most of his life. Bai Honghu began her writing career in 1940. This story, the Chinese title of which is *A Mengbie Girl*, is from Bai Honghu's 1978 collection of short stories. The story itself has been included as one of the stories in the American publication *Anthology of International Short Stories* (No. 24, 1981). Yang Zhao has tried his hand at most literary forms: short stories, prose, reportage and literary criticism. The most successful ones have been these recent ones, written in collaboration with his wife.

Bai Honghu and Yang Zhao
Hansuai, the Living Ghost

Aijuad's and Hansuai's rooms faced each other on either side of the garden, in which lay a pond encircled with banyan and fruit-laden papaya trees. From time to time Aijuad would interrupt his studies to stare at Hansuai from his window. Through her window, he saw her erect figure by the lamp, as she concentrated on writing down the figures with one hand, while calculating with the abacus with the other.

Hansuai always studied diligently and was one of the top students in her class. At first, Aijuad had found calculating with the abacus difficult, though he could recite mathematical tables fluently, but Hansuai had never laughed at him.

'Just use this and don't be afraid,' she said, pointing to her head to encourage him. 'The more you use your brains the sharper they become.'

Whenever Aijuad looked at Hansuai's lighted window, he was encouraged.

One afternoon, the students were going to see a film. Aijuad had never seen Hansuai go out or see a film. When he met her he asked, 'Are you going to the film, Hansuai?'

'Me?—I haven't made up my mind yet.'

'Why not?'

She was silent.

'You should go. I was intending to do some washing, but Comrade Aifuang said the film is a very good one. Studying isn't the only way to learn. Films can teach you something too.'

'OK, I'll go then.'

On reaching the cinema, Aijuad searched everywhere for Hansuai, but couldn't find her. Why hadn't she come?

142

Before the film ended, he left the cinema and hurried to Hansuai's room. No one was there. Through the window he looked into the garden and spotted Hansuai squatting by the pond, washing a man's headdress in a basin. Aijuad wondered to whom it belonged. Then as she lathered it, he noticed a sky-blue stain on it. It was his. He had carelessly spilt ink on it the previous day.

Eagerly, he ran out of the room and, turning a corner, rushed to Hansuai shouting, 'Hansuai! Hansuai!'

With her head bent over her washing, she was startled to see Aijuad. Raising her eyes, she asked, 'Has the film finished already?'

'Why didn't you go to the film? Why stay here and wash my clothes instead?'

'Look, silly! I was doing my own washing, so I thought I'd do yours too. You're so busy with your studies. I can wash quicker than you.'

Aijuad found there were many clothes in the basin, not just his but those of other friends too. Rolling up his sleeves, he squatted down beside her. 'Let's do them together.' So saying, he took some clothes and began scrubbing one of them, a skirt of Hansuai's.

Feeling embarrassed, she tried to snatch it back. 'Put it down! Put it down!'

Looking at the skirt in his hand, Aijuad smiled, not minding a bit. 'Calm down! If you can wash our clothes, why can't we wash yours?' He glanced at her affectionately.

Their eyes met, so that she turned hastily away. Her manner suddenly grew cool and she fixed her eyes on the ground as if preoccupied with some problem. After a while, she picked up her basin and went away without a word.

Looking at her retreating figure, Aijuad was puzzled. She was as beautiful as a flower, yet as cold as stone. Back in his room, his emotions were confused. When the other students returned from the film, laughing and talking, he went to see Aifuang, the dean of the Nationalities' Cadre School and secretary of the Youth League branch of the accountancy training class. Aijuad told him abruptly, 'Hansuai is so good.

She doesn't just help us in our studies, but also in our daily lives. She was washing our clothes today. I think we should admit her into the Youth League.'

Whatever the problem, Aifuang was never at a loss. But now he frowned and was silent for a long time, before sighing.

'What's the matter? Have I said something wrong?' Aijuad asked.

'Of course not! That's a good suggestion. We should try to help her, but it will take time. Now, how are you getting on in your studies? Any difficulties?' he said, changing the subject.

Since Aijuad had not come to talk about this, he soon left.

After that, Aijuad began to watch Hansuai's behaviour more closely. She was a strange contradiction of modesty and friendliness and unreasoning stubbornness. She would gaily chat in class and then snub everyone afterwards.

One fine Sunday morning, the students were up early and hurrying to go home or out. Aijuad watched while Hansuai took her time having breakfast. As always, she clearly wasn't going anywhere. He walked over and said, 'Won't you go home today?'

'No.'

'Where do you live?'

'Oh, far away,' she replied.

'Then come to my home instead and meet my family.'

'No, thank you.'

'Come on! My family live in Manliu Village near the town. There's no need to be so formal.'

When he tried to take her arm, she dodged away with a curious look, declining his invitation in a proud and bitter tone. As she ran away, he noticed there were tears in her eyes. Since he was now in no mood to go home, he went to see Aifuang again. He began, 'Hansuai seems to have some problems.'

'How do you know that?' the dean asked in astonishment, his composure shaken.

'I feel it.'

With a deep frown, Aifuang sighed.

'Really, Comrade Aifuang! Whenever I mention Hansuai,

you just sigh!'

As if he had not heard him, Aifuang moved nearer to Aijuad and stared at him. 'Isn't your home in Manliu Village?' he asked.

'Yes.'

'And how many are in your family?'

'Only two. My mother and I.'

'What's your mother like?'

'She works very hard.'

The dean nodded. 'Are there many superstitious people in your village?' he continued after a pause.

'Of course. Too many!' Not quite understanding the line of questioning, Aijuad added, 'A lot of them believe that illness is caused by ghost people. Once when I was sick, my mother pricked my chest with a tiger's fang and muttered to herself, "Which village are you from, you evil ghost? What's your name? Tell me or I'll stab you with this tiger's fang." Then she pricked me until I bled.'

'Have you ever seen any ghost people?'

'Yes. It was the year before Liberation, and I was just over fifteen then. I saw a male living ghost being driven out of a village near ours. He brought his wife and two children with him. On the orders of the chief, he sacrificed a cock to the gods at the crossroads. Kneeling on the ground, he made a pledge that he and his family would live far away and never return, even when they became real ghosts at their deaths. . . .'

Aifuang's expression was furious. Cutting Aijuad short, he demanded, 'Is that man a human being or a ghost person?'

'A human being of course!'

'Then you've never seen any ghosts?'

'Never! Who could see a ghost?'

'Are there any ghosts?'

'No, of course not!'

Back in his room Aijuad realized that he was still in a dilemma over Hansuai. Why had Aifuang talked to him about living ghosts? Was it possible that . . ? He dared not think any longer. His heart pounded. Such thoughts were ridiculous!

2

Filled with suspicion, Aijuad tried to find out where Hansuai lived, but she seldom chatted after class, especially with him. Whenever he approached she would avoid him.

It was early in April that the accountancy training class ended. The day after the graduation ceremony, the students would return home, so Aijuad was very anxious to have a talk with Hansuai. It had not been easy for them to study, since both came from poor families. But for Liberation this would not have been possible. Even if they were not to be close friends, he hoped they could at least keep in touch. That afternoon he saw her packing, alone in her room. Going over he said:

'How time flies! Half a year has passed in a flash.'

Like a deer, Hansuai was flustered to see him. Controlling herself a little, she murmured, 'Yes.'

Sitting down Aijuad watched her packing. 'We've studied and learnt how to calculate with an abacus.'

'And how to develop these border areas.'

'Exactly! Back home in our villages we must do all we can.'

'We'll work for better harvests too.'

Hansuai was rather reserved at first, but the more they talked the more ardent and intimate they became. The afternoon passed until it was almost time for supper. Aijuad went on in high spirits:

'I'm so happy for the future of us Dais.'

'And I'm so happy for the people of my village.'

'Aren't your people Dais?' Aijuad asked puzzled.

'No. They . . . they aren't!' she retorted, her voice rising.

'Where is your village then?' he pressed, hoping to solve the mystery.

'Here on earth, in the world of men! It's a fascinating place, better than anywhere else.' Although she praised her village, there was no happiness in her tone. It was as if she was arguing a case.

'So where is this paradise?' Aijuad tried to ascertain.

'Oh, it's getting late. Come on! Let's go to the office. There's so much to be done before we leave tomorrow.'

She changed the subject, her face grave. Turning round she

walked away before Aijuad could say anything more, leaving her clothes scattered on her bed.

The next morning, the graduates were about to set off for home, scurrying about bidding each other farewell. Aijuad knew Hansuai would neither come to say goodbye to him nor expect him to say it to her. Walking to a huge banyan tree outside the gate, he stood hoping to see her once more before they parted. She appeared carrying two bamboo crates on a shoulder-pole. She walked slowly, her head down, her eyes misty. As she passed him her pace quickened, but at the bend of the road by a coconut palm she turned round to glance at him. Looking after her, Aijuad forgot that he too must leave for home. After she had disappeared into the distance, he went to see the dean once more.

With tears in his eyes, he asked where Hansuai lived. Instead of answering, the dean asked him why he wanted to know her address. Aijuad urged him to tell, but the dean just replied, 'Now let things be. You run off home immediately.'

'No, I won't!' declared Aijuad.

'Why not?'

'She's so mysterious. There's something troubling her. I want to find out the truth or I'll never have any peace of mind.'

'Young men should be light-hearted, not so heavy.'

'Comrade Aifuang, you kept her secret while she was still a student. But why won't you tell me the truth now that she has left? Must I be kept in the dark all my life?'

His sad face reminded Aifuang of another's, which had appeared six months previously, on the last day of registration for the accountancy training class.

A slender girl had entered, wearing a light green top and bright blue skirt. Pretty and intelligent-looking, she glanced around uneasily, her eyes sparkling. When the clerk asked from which village she came, she blushed and answered, 'From Mengjang district.'

'Yes, but which village?'

'From Mengjang district!' she insisted, as if defending herself.

Overhearing her arguing, Aifuang invited her into a vacant office and asked, 'Is your name Hansuai?'

'Yes,' she answered, raising her head puzzled.

'You can tell him the name of your village.'

'No, I won't.' She lowered her head again, biting her lips.

'Why not?'

'Because I won't tell anyone except a Communist Party member.'

'Who do you think I am?'

The girl raised her head again. In spite of his cadre's uniform, one could tell he was a Dai from his face, even without hearing his pure Dai dialect. She scrutinized him, while she nervously fingered her skirt.

'As a Dai and a Party member, I understand your dilemma. But we've been liberated and those terrible dark days have gone for ever. You must believe that things have changed. Others won't judge you as before and you shouldn't expect the worst from others.'

Although he talked with her for a long time, she kept her head down and said stubbornly, 'I've nothing more to say. I'm here to study for my people, that's all!'

He talked with her often about her studies, and she would beam with joy and talk animatedly. But the moment he touched on her personal life, she would stubbornly clam up, 'I've nothing more to say!'

She seldom left the school grounds.

Recalling this, Aifuang paced the room in agitation, stopping at last in front of Aijuad. Patting him on the shoulder he sighed, 'She's very unfortunate. No need to increase her pain.'

'Please tell me the truth.'

'She . . . she's from Mengbie Village . . .'

Aijuad felt a shiver go down his spine. Mengbie Village? That's where the living ghosts lived before Liberation. Only after Liberation, it had got a name.

'I can't believe it. She . . . she's a good girl . . .' His voice trembled so that he couldn't continue. No, it wasn't true! Hansuai from Mengbie Village! The fond dream he had hoped would come true a moment ago of Hansuai and he marrying and working together in the same co-operative suddenly turned into a nightmare. He visualized his friendly relatives and neighbours cursing and sneering at Hansuai, his mother refusing to agree to their marriage. Aijuad was deeply upset.

As if he had read his mind, Aifuang said, 'Hansuai is a good girl and all the Mengbie villagers are good too.' Then he added, 'Have you ever seen a village headman being accused of being a living ghost? No, all the accused were peasants!'

Aijuad began to understand what Aifuang was saying, and so staring at the dean, he listened carefully filled with grief and indignation.

'There is no such thing as a ghost,' Aifuang emphasized. 'For example, take Hansuai's mother. About thirty years ago, when she was a beautiful teenager, she lived with her parents in Mangbang Village, which had been their home for generations. The headman was a known womanizer and wanted to seduce her. At dusk one day, when she was on her way to husk rice, he jumped out from his hiding-place in a bamboo grove near the river and tried to embrace her. Although she looked frail, she was strong and slapped his face so hard that he staggered back. After that he hated her and planned his revenge. Later that summer, a woman transplanting rice seedlings fell ill with malaria. The headman started the rumour that Hansuai's mother had gone to the sick woman's home to borrow a bamboo crate and that her ghost had caused the illness. On the orders of the wicked headman, their hut was burnt and they were driven out of the village.'

Aijuad cried out, 'Why doesn't the government issue a law stating that there are no living ghosts and that it is against the law to brand a person as one?'

Shaking his head, Aifuang explained, 'That wouldn't do. People must get rid of these ideas themselves. You asked me twice about Hansuai's past, but I didn't tell you because I was afraid you'd look down on her and discriminate against her.'

Aijuad hung his head in shame. Although he didn't believe in ghosts, he hadn't known the reasons why people were branded as such. If only he had known earlier, he could have helped Hansuai. How childish and ignorant he had been!

3

After leaving the dean's room, Aijuad set off for Mengbie Village, walking quickly hoping to catch up with Hansuai.

Mengbie Village was far away in a valley at the foot of a mountain. On the way, Aijuad passed many villages, fields, ridges and streams. The further he went the fewer villages and the more rugged the path. The area, formerly a wild forest, was the haunt of tigers and leopards. As more and more living ghosts were banished there, they set up their village, clearing the forest. As Aijuad walked along the rough mountain path, he thought of those wretched people who had dragged themselves along that same way, just as Hansuai's mother and her grandmother had. They must have suffered deeply. But for the Communist Party and Liberation, they would have endured those injustices for ever, leading the life of outcasts from generation to generation, while more and more victims were driven there.

He lost all sense of time. Suddenly the path broadened with neat rows of banyan trees lining it like bright trellises. Among the luscious green grass colourful wild flowers ran riot. The surface of the pools mirrored the blue sky and the white geese. Golden wheat grew in abundance. There was beauty and tranquility wherever one looked. Aijuad's eyes drank in the beauty. Expecting to arrive at Mengbie Village soon, he wondered what it would be like and how the people were.

Suddenly he spotted a girl emerge from a wheat field. It was Hansuai! Her eyes sparkled with joy at the good harvest. Aijuad rushed towards her, taking her hand and saying, 'Hello, Hansuai! I followed you here!'

Hansuai was delighted to see him, but she was uncertain what he meant. Why had he followed her?

While she had been a student, Aijuad had often been in her thoughts. He was warm-hearted and honest, an idealistic young man. She had become very fond of him and sensed he was in love with her. But whenever she thought about their future, her joy was overshadowed by her past.

As a child, she had not known there was such discrimination. When selling eggs at the fairs, the boys had buzzed around her like bees round a honey-pot, singing love songs and competing with one another for her attentions. She ignored them all. One day when she went to the market, the boys began to swarm around her as always, singing until their throats ached. Hansuai smiled. Suddenly a voice rang out, 'She's from Mengbie Village! A living ghost!' The boys' faces registered horror as they fled in panic.

Heart-broken, Hansuai sobbed out her story in her mother's arms when she reached home.

Indignantly her mother said, 'Ignore them, Hansuai. We live in Mengbie Village. Let the rest of the world go by!'

From that time, Hansuai's heart was heavy and she swore never to leave the village again. After Liberation, however, there were the movements to give the land back to the peasants and set up co-operatives. She was chosen by the district administration to learn accounting, but she refused, afraid of persecution. 'I won't go,' she protested. 'We can run the co-operative well without any accountants.'

The Party secretary of the district committee had at last persuaded her and so she had entered the Nationalities' Cadre School. There she seldom went out in case someone recognized her, and kept her distance from her classmates in case they discovered about her past. She was afraid they would sneer at her if they knew the truth. As for Aijuad, he was a sincere friend, but she was sure that if he knew, he would abandon her and break her heart. Whenever she thought of this she trembled.

Now Aijuad had come to her! Had the Communist Party really destroyed superstition? Had she misjudged Aijuad?

Seeing her bewildered expression. Aijuad tried to reassure her, 'This new society has given us Dai people a new life!'

Touched, she replied, 'How did you find me?'

'Comrade Aifuang told me everything so I decided to come after you.'

Hansuai was deeply grateful to Aifuang, who had told her

many times not to expect the worst from others. Yet she still was uncertain if Aijuad was really as determined as he declared.

'How could you love such an unfortuante girl as me?'

'The past is past. Now we have a new life, a new beginning, a new way of thinking,' Aijuad said, hugging Hansuai.

A pair of swans rose from the pool, flapping their wings and soaring into the blue sky.

1953

Translated by Hu Shiguang

Ji Xuepei

He was born in Henan province in 1926. Due to difficult family circumstances, he received a rather haphazard education but managed to get into the Normal Middle School in Luoyang in his home province. He had to discontinue his studies after only four months because there was no money.

After 1949 he taught in a primary school in Henan and began writing in his spare time. His published works include: a volume of poetry, the collections of prose *Morning* and *Waves*; seven collections of short stories, among them *Two Brigade Leaders*; a novella and a biography. He has also written for children.

Ji Xuepei

Two Brigade Leaders

Aunt Wei's sheep were nibbling the young wheat of the brigade, when Liu Kuaihuo, who was in charge of keeping work-points, caught them. According to regulations, a fine of one yuan would be imposed for each sheep that had caused the damage.

He also realized that there would be one hell of a rumpus over this.

Aunt Wei was the village's notorious harpy. In arithmetic, for example, she couldn't count more than a hundred. But when she was arguing, she could hold her own with anyone and brazen it out for days and nights if necessary. Everyone was afraid of her and had nicknamed her the 'Village Terror'.

Kuaihuo was not in the least afraid of her. Although he was a mere seventeen and still had a youthful smile on his face, he was quite grown-up and had a good head on his shoulders. 'Every family has taken good care of its sheep, since we worked out those rules,' he thought to himself. 'But our village Terror has ignored them all. If we let her get away with it this time, no one will bother any more about the rules. All right. She's stuck her neck out, so let it get chopped. We'll make an example of her.'

He took the two sheep to the brigade office, where the deputy brigade leader, Liu Quanyou was the only one. In excitement, the boy cried out as he entered the gate: 'Look, deputy brigade leader! I've caught some thieves!'

Though in his fifties, Liu looked older and was a bit of an old woman in his ways. Concentrating on repairing a cart and with his back to the gate, he was startled by Kuaihuo's voice and demanded quickly: 'What thieves?'

Kuaihuo winked and, making a face at the sheep, burst out laughing. 'These two. They sneaked into the northern wheat field and were grazing to their hearts' content. See what a bellyful they've had!'

Liu relaxed and examined the animals. Their bellies were as fat as gourds, their teeth stained green. They certainly seemed to have had a good time. Then he asked, 'Aren't these Aunt Wei's pride and joy?'

'I don't give a damn whose they are!' Kuaihuo retorted. 'They ate the brigade's wheat, so the fine should be imposed.' So saying, he tied the sheep to an old elm tree.

Liu sighed, very irritated, and in his heart he reproached the youth, 'Kuaihuo, my boy, you've really loused things up. Why must you force a confrontation with such a character? When she hears about this, she'll kick up one hell of a fuss . . .'

He'd hardly had time to say the words aloud when the Village Terror's piercing voice could be heard crying outside, '. . . Who the devil was it? Just itching to make trouble, eh? What have my little pets done? You wait. Granny's going to sort you out right now!'

Seeing the situation was getting too hot for comfort, Liu told Kuaihuo hastily, 'Tell her none of us cadres is here,' as he ran into the northern room in retreat.

Kuaihuo didn't know whether to laugh or be angry. But knowing how timid Liu was, he just tightened his belt and waited for the Village Terror to descend on him.

She came rushing in like a gust of wind, a group of eager little boys and girls tagging along behind her hoping to see some fun. About forty and short in stature, she had a flat face. Her eyebrows were creased in a furious frown; her mouth pouting.

Kuaihuo took a few steps backwards, ready for her attack. But it was quite unnecessary. When she saw Kuaihuo was the only person around, she didn't deign to give him a second glance but swaggered over to untether her sheep.

'Hey, wait a moment!' Kuaihuo protested, trying to stop her. 'You can't take them away like that!'

'Mind your own business!' she snapped at him.

Biting his lip, the youth smiled and asked, 'So you think the brigade grows wheat just for your sheep to eat?'

'To hell with it!' cried the woman. 'My sheep have been safely in my yard. How could they have eaten the wheat? What a rotten accusation!'

'So these sheep aren't yours?'

'What do you mean? Why aren't they mine?'

'Because I caught them in the northern field. How could they be yours then?'

Getting more worked up, the Village Terror moved a step nearer to the boy and asked, 'What's the matter with you, Kuaihuo? Why are you trying to make trouble? Have I thrown your darling baby into the well or something?'

'Hardly! I haven't even a wife yet,' he smiled. 'You know very well it's a question of principle.'

Having failed to talk him over, the Village Terror now tried to threaten him. 'Are you going to let me take them home or not?'

'Of course, but not until the brigade leader comes back.'

'Then your granny will have to fight you.' With this she tried to push the youth, but Kuaihuo dodged away from her and caught hold of the rope tethering the sheep. She tried desperately to wrest the rope from him.

The crowd of children were delighted. Jumping up and down with glee they shouted: 'Hold on, Brother Kuaihuo! Don't let go!'

'Sure! A fat chance she's got!' the older boy laughed.

Beaten, the Village Terror gave up. Then she began roaming around the courtyard, clapping her hands and crying: 'Where are our cadres? Where are those damn village cadres? Good grief! How could you cadres egg on this little twerp to bully me?' She began searching the room for the cadres.

Kuaihuo seized this chance to tell a plump boy to go and fetch Uncle Zhenqi from the eastern pit. 'Make it snappy!' he ordered.

The little boy gave a triumphant whoop and led his playmates away.

After a while the Village Terror emerged from the northern

room. It was incredible, but she'd failed to find Liu there. Reluctant to accept her defeat, she shrieked at Kuaihuo, 'Just you wait! I'll fetch the brigade leaders and settle accounts with you, my lad!' then she strode off in a fury.

Kuaihuo wasn't in the least cowed and shouted back cheerfully, 'OK. The sooner the better!'

Then Liu emerged from the room, his head and back covered in dust. Kuaihuo burst out laughing. Liu, frowning, scolded, 'Oh shit! What a bloody row you've caused!'

'Don't blame me,' Kuaihuo protested. 'I didn't make the rules. They were worked out by our brigade members.'

Liu pointed his finger at the boy. 'You ought to understand more about the spirit of making regulations.' He continued after a pause, 'We just want to encourage people to look after their sheep. It's not really necessary to impose a fine on them, I feel. Don't you see that?'

Puzzled, Kuaihuo smiled and asked, 'But what if they don't bother to look after their sheep?'

'It's up to their conscience.'

'But Aunt Wei didn't bother and broke the rules . . .'

'Oh, she's only one individual,' Liu quibbled.

'But tell me,' Kuaihuo insisted, 'what should we do with this particular individual?'

'Well, we could do this,' Liu answered after a moment's thought. 'You take the sheep back to her and tell her off so that she won't be so careless again.'

'That's no good! If we overlook the regulations this time, everyone will ignore them in future. The wheat shoots have just grown, and there are a lot of sheep in the village. What if other sheep damage the wheat?' He stopped for a moment, thinking to himself, 'If we let our Village Terror off so easily now, it will mean we sacrifice the principle and the interests of the collective.'

Kuaihuo was an honest and straightforward youth. He would never insist on something unless he was sure about it. 'You'd better go yourself and give her back her sheep. I'm not good at theorizing. I wouldn't know how to make her see reason.'

Like a scalded cat, Liu jumped backwards and said hurriedly, 'No, no! You're just the person to do the job. After all, you know the old saying, "Let the one who tied the bell untie it."'

It suddenly dawned on Kuaihuo, 'Liu never wants to offend anyone.'

Just then, the Village Terror was heard yelling in the distance. Liu advised, 'Let her have her way, if she comes for the sheep.'

Determinedly Kuaihuo caught hold of his arm, 'If she comes, then you can give her a strong criticism.'

'No, you'd better do that. I've got something very important to attend to.' With that he struggled free and fled into the room again.

But it was a false alarm. The person who entered was none other than Liu Zhenqi, the brigade leader.

He was a simple, honest and robust-looking man in his early thirties. He always seemed to be very cheerful and alert.

Kuaihuo was delighted. 'Thank goodness you've come at last.'

'Having a bit of difficulty, eh?' he grinned as he approached. 'You were quite right to catch the sheep and bring them here. If we hadn't caught her sheep at it this time, it might have become a tricky situation to tackle. The sheep have damaged quite a large area of wheat.'

'You've been there already?' asked Kuaihuo.

'Of course,' Zhenqi sighed. Then he inquired if Liu was in.

Kuaihuo gestured with his chin in the direction of the room and whispered, 'He wants me to give her back the sheep.'

'But has she admitted she was in the wrong?'

'What? Some hopes you have of that!' Kuaihuo pulled a face. 'She created such a racket, we thought all hell had been let loose.'

'Then why should we give her back her sheep?'

At this Liu came out and started to drag Zhenqi into the room, whispering in a low voice: 'Quickly! I've got something important to tell you.'

Inside the room Liu began to explain, 'You know, Zhenqi

what an old bitch our Village Terror is. If we handle this affair badly, she'll make such a commotion that our production will be affected and others will accuse us cadres of not uniting our brigade members. So I think . . . we'd better . . . er . . . treat the affair as a small one and let her off . . .'

Zhenqi cut him short: 'And if the others follow her fine example?'

'My dear nephew,' Liu began, patting Zhenqi on the shoulder, 'you can count them on one finger. Is there anyone else in our village like that old witch?'

Zhenqi chuckled: 'What a splendid idea of yours! Return the sheep with our sincere apologies, then everything will be just fine. Really, uncle, do you think our brigade members will thank us for that?'

'But we can explain what happened, can't we?' After a while he continued: 'Perhaps I shouldn't be so frank, but there is an old saying, "To offend a person is to build a wall in front of you." We won't remain cadres all our lives and . . .'

'So according to you cadres should be useless and ineffectual.' Then Zhenqi asked sharply, 'Why should our villagers have entrusted us with the job of cadre?'

Ashamed, Liu coughed.

'I can't accept your advice, uncle,' Zhenqi replied seriously. 'It would mean sacrificing the interests of our collective just to keep in that old hag's good books. According to you, we should try to keep in with everyone, but that doesn't work. Moreover you're just thinking of your self and not of the collective, and that is no answer. I'd rather risk her wrath than smooth things over.'

Liu blushed deeply and scratched his neck, muttering nervously, 'OK forget what I've just said. But I'm telling you, you'll have a tough job on your hands trying to make that old hag see sense.'

'We can only try. After all she's human, not stone.'

Just then Kuaihuo burst into the room shouting, 'She's coming!' They went out to find her already in the courtyard. The moment she saw the two cadres she rushed forward waving her hands and shrieking, 'Oh, my good cadres! I'm so unfortunate! My two sheep were safe in the yard, but someone tried to cause trouble and accuse me. But you're just, you can settle the matter.'

Liu stepped back and began coughing.

Zhenqi remained where he was, smiling. He said nothing but simply let her talk. Puzzled by this, she stopped and asked in dismay, 'Well, why the hell don't you say something?'

Immediately Zhenqi told Kuaihuo to fetch a chair for Aunt Wei.

The boy was a little surprised, but, sensing the situation, rushed into the office and returned with a large armchair, which he placed in front of her. 'My good aunt,' he began, 'you must be exhausted with all your rushing about. Please sit down here.'

Then Zhenqi gave another order, 'Please bring us some tea, Kuaihuo.'

'Right away!' said the boy and he quickly produced some cups and a pot of tea.

Zhenqi politely asked Aunt Wei to sit down as he served her some tea. She was bewildered and at a loss as to what to do. After they had urged her several times, she finally sat down. Holding the cup she was too nervous to drink.

Bringing out two benches, Zhenqi and the others then sat down. Lingering over his cup of tea, Zhenqi slowly began with a smile, 'We rarely have the chance to talk over things, so please don't spare your comments if you have any criticisms about our work.'

Aunt Wei had been in a rage when she had arrived at the office, determined to give them a piece of her mind. But now, in the circumstances, she felt the wind had been taken out of her sails. Not knowing what to say, she stared at her tea-cup and muttered vaguely, 'Oh, things are all right so far.'

'Then do you think we were right to adopt that regulation about the wheat field?'

Silence.

'Do you think we were right?' Zhenqi pressed her.

'Yes.'

'I can see you're a reasonable person. Have some tea,' Zhenqi encouraged her. Taking a sip from his cup and then wiping his mouth with his hand, he continued, 'When did we adopt those regulations?' He stopped abruptly as if forgetting the date.

'The night of 4th November,' Kuaihuo eagerly butted in.

'Of course, you're right!' Zhenqi agreed, carefully watching Aunt Wei's expression. 'Now I remember. You were at the meeting that night, Aunt Wei, weren't you? In fact you voted for those regulations, didn't you?'

'Yes, they were adopted unanimously,' Kuaihuo said taking the cue, afraid she would try to deny it.

Aunt Wei said nothing. Then after a while she broke her silence and said with a determined toss of her head, 'Anyway, my sheep were safe in the yard.'

Kuaihuo was about to reply, when Zhenqi stopped him and asked with a smile, 'If that was the case, how did they get into the wheat field?'

'Who knows? They've legs, haven't they?'

Kuaihuo roared with laughter, while Zhenqi pressed his advantage: 'So you admit they ate the wheat shoots?'

Aunt Wei pursed her lips and took a deep breath.

'Since it was your sheep that damaged the crop, what have you to say?' asked Zhenqi after a pause.

She glanced at him and countered, 'Well, what do you have to say first?'

'I say,' Zhenqi began with a grin and holding up two fingers, 'that according to the rules, you are fined two yuan.'

'Then I give up. I'll pay.' She put down her cup and went over to untie her sheep.

Liu couldn't help smiling and whispered in Zhenqi's ear, 'Well done! You've beaten her at last.'

Zhenqi looked at Liu and said meaningfully, 'Cadres should not be afraid to offend people to see justice done.'

Kuaihuo didn't bother about what they were saying. Lost in his thoughts he smiled to himself and said, 'Our brigade leader is terrific!'

Translated by Wen Xue

Sun Yuchun

One of the youngest of these writers, Sun Yuchun, was born in 1947, in Anhui province. A graduate of a secondary school that specializes in literary pursuits, he has worked as an editor of literary publications and has also spent some time as a labourer. Indeed, he was already writing while still in secondary school and had a number of poems published at that time. He is now a journalist with the *Workers' Daily*. In the last ten years or so, he has had many poems and essays published as well as ten short stories and a novella. *In Vino Veritas* was published in *Anhui Literature* in April 1979.

Sun Yuchun

In Vino Veritas

A few dishes, a wine cup and a pair of chopsticks were laid out on the red sandalwood table. Erxi had just poured himself out some wine when a man entered. Raising his head, he said in surprise, 'Ah, Secretary Guo!'

Guo Shichang, the commune's Party secretary, stood with a foot either side of the doorway. Surveying the scene, he chortled and said, 'Ha! You're in a good mood today. Drinking by yourself, eh? Where's your wife?'

'Gone to see her mother.' The worried frown on Erxi's face vanished, as he went to the kitchen to fetch another cup and pair of chopsticks. Filling the cup with wine, he remarked, 'You're a rare visitor, Secretary Guo! Have a drink.'

Guo did not refuse. Plumping down in a chair, he picked up the wine bottle to examine it and said, 'Whew! So even your tiny village has famous wines like this. That's good!' He drained the cup in one gulp. 'A fine wine! Excellent!' he praised, as he wiped his mouth with his plump hand. Then he popped some fried peanuts into his mouth. 'I've come to apologize to you, Erxi. You know me well. I've been a cadre too long . . . How old are you now?'

'Twenty-seven, going on twenty-eight.'

'Of course! When I became a cadre, you were still a twinkle in your father's eye! With the years it's hard to avoid becoming bureaucratic. Take now. I don't mind your putting up big-character posters criticizing me. After all, it's in the constitution. Everyone can speak out his views and argue. It was wrong to have you locked up, especially when you had just got married. I didn't know about it then. But that doesn't matter.

Still, however you look at it. I was responsible. These few days I've been thinking it over. I realized that your criticisms are fair. You were quite right.'

Erxi was simple and näive. He had no idea about flattery and hypocrisy. When he spoke he was rather shy. His mother thought him inarticulate and his father-in-law disliked his reticence. His wife often reproached him, 'What's the matter? Have you lost your tongue?'

Hearing Guo's words, Erxi didn't know how to reply but he felt certain that he meant what he said. Since the land reform Secretary Guo had been very powerful in this part of the country. Every word he said counted. No one could challenge his authority. But now he was personally apologizing to a humble team leader. That was the style of an old cadre. When the Party called for more democracy, he dropped his pretentious airs. With these thoughts, Erxi poured out another cup for Guo and said respectfully, 'Drink another cup, Secretary Guo!'

Guo drank three cups in a row and then took out a cigarette to light. Suddenly he chucked it at Erxi and took out another for himself. Flurried and blushing a little, Erxi pushed it back, saying he did not smoke. Then seeing Guo relax, puffing at his cigarette, Erxi began cautiously, 'Secretary Guo . . . My mother said I had too many opinions and my father-in-law felt I was just showing off. But in fact they both supported the posters. You can't plant rape on low-lying land. Last year we lost everything, including the seeds. This year again you've given instructions about planting it. Isn't it as clear as day that we'll suffer?'

Guo chewed a piece of meat and mumbled, 'Yes, we only paid attention to class struggle these past years. Not enough to production. We made arbitrary decisions and gave orders blindly. Even used coercion where . . .' Suddenly he spat with disgust, for he had chewed some aniseed by mistake, and took a gulp of wine, Erxi apologetically searched the dish for the aniseed. Seeing the secretary intent on drinking, Erxi took up the thread of the conversation, 'Yes, the commune members have suffered a lot. Dried sweet potatoes are our staple food.

We used to sell eggs to make a little pocket money on the side. When rearing hens was forbidden, that put a stop to that. Life was even harder. I often asked myself if we would have to eat sweet potatoes all our lives. I wondered why we couldn't plant rice on the low ground. Now it will be better. Everyone's happy that the production teams have the right to decide what to plant. Next year if we don't get a bumper harvest, I'll crawl on my hands and knees backwards round Toad Canal three times . . . Cheers! Secretary Guo!' As he was speaking his mind, Erxi became more eloquent.

Another three cups later, Guo's face turned red and his forehead shone with perspiration. Unbuttoning his jacket, he felt talkative and began slowly, 'Erxi, I don't want to criticize you again, but after two cups of wine, you wouldn't know that a pan is made of iron. You young people don't care if you make fools of yourselves boasting. How can you be sure of getting a bumper harvest next year if you decide what to plant? Thirty years I've been a leader, yet I still haven't got rid of our poverty. But you brag away. Don't you have any respect for us old cadres? Of course you're young still, only in your twenties. When I was your age, I didn't fear anything either. I was like a rebel in the *Outlaws of the Marsh*.[1] Even the earth trembled when I stamped!'

He paused for a while and then pointed at the table. 'Take this table, for example,' he continued. 'It was me who distributed it during the land reform, wasn't it? A hero doesn't brag about his past though. Now the Party tells us to be more democratic. You think I don't know what that means? But you've got some queer ideas. You think it means putting up wall posters against your leaders and kicking up a fuss! That's all wrong! You may have democracy, but I have centralism!' The more he spoke the angrier he became, banging the table with his chopsticks. Erxi became more and more bewildered as he listened, wondering what the commune Party secretary was driving at.

Seeing Erxi's puzzled look, Guo again remembered the

1. An ancient Chinese novel about a peasant uprising.

purpose of his visit. He lowered his voice. 'I don't want you to land in trouble, so I'm warning you. A handful of trouble-makers are using the word democracy to stir things up. Don't let yourself play into their hands. It will be too late to feel sorry if that happens!'

He helped himself to another drink, and then filled his cup again before Erxi could pour one out for him.

Clutching his chopsticks, Erxi was in a daze, as he gradually realized that Guo had not come to make a sincere apology, and that the right to decide about production was an illusion. Frowning, he said nothing more.

After finishing that cup, Guo hiccuped three times. His face turned from red to yellow. Erxi, afraid Guo was getting so plastered that he would do something stupid, suggested, 'You've had a lot to drink, Secretary Guo. Why not lie down on the bed and have a rest?'

'Not yet.' And just to prove that he wasn't drunk, Guo lifted his head and downed another cup of wine. After holding the cup to his lips, he took it away, wanting to refill it. But as the bottle was empty, he threw the cup on the table. It rolled along the edge and smashed to the floor before Erxi could catch it.

As if he'd been slapped, Erxi's face grew hot and he stood awkwardly at the table, staring at Guo. The secretary hiccuped again and scratched himself. He was really tipsy. 'In Vino Veritas,' as the saying goes. Now Guo struck the table and spoke out what was on his mind.

'You really think I came here to apologize to you, Jiang Erxi? Shit! I wouldn't give you that honour! But Secretary Zhou of the county Party committee criticized me strongly and forced me to come. Otherwise I wouldn't touch your bloody wine! Hell! You think your little posters scared me? What crap! I don't give a damn about ten thousand posters, let alone your eight or ten! During the Cultural Revolution, there were posters everywhere, but no one touched a hair of my head. You're too eager to get the right to decide. Too big for your boots! You demand this right and that right. That means seizing power from the working class! But if you get all the power, what about me? I know what'll happen if I give you the right to

decide today. Give you an inch and you'll take a mile! . . .
Democracy? Shit! Yes, I mean it. You can go to the county Party
committee and tell Zhou Yun what I, Guo Shichang, said. If you
want . . . power, go . . . and stick up your po—posters . . . '

Erxi was choked with anger while tears welled up in his
eyes. He thought, 'You often said fine words, but in fact your
ideas stink!' Now he realized it would not be easy to achieve
democracy. One simply could not rely on democracy bestowed
as a favour. In fact, democracy was not yet within his reach.
Swallowing his wine in one mouthful he replied decisively,
'Yes, I'll certainly write more posters!'

His quiet defiance sobered Guo up a bit. Shooting a sidelong
glance at Erxi who refused to be intimidated, Guo lost his
temper and bellowed, 'All right! Just you dare stick up another
poster and sabotage the country's stability and unity. I'll have
you arrested! Go ahead and try it!' Then supported by the
table, he rose unsteadily to his feet and staggered out,
muttering, 'Don't think I can't squash you. Otherwise being a
cadre for th—thirty years means nothing. J—just wait and see,
you snotty little twerp!'

Erxi sat motionless at the table strewn with empty dishes
and chopsticks. 'There is no use getting angry,' he thought.
'What is to be done now?' He began thinking seriously.

Translated by Wu Liang

Liu Fudao

Liu Fudao, who was born in Hubei, central China, in 1940, spent three years as a teacher of primary and secondary students before entering the army in 1962. His work in the army was in fact a lead-in to his writing since his were not so much regular army duties, but newspaper work and other cultural activities. Liu Fudao's permanent job is as a specialist in these fields with the People's Liberation Army. He began his literary pursuits with the publication of some short stories and essays in 1972. One of these stories, *Spectacles* and this story, *Moon over the South Lake*, won prizes separately as superior stories of the years 1978 and 1980. *Moon over the South Lake* was published in *People's Literature* No. 7, 1980. It reflects some of the problems that existed in certain enterprises at the time and which are now in the process of being resolved.

Liu Fudao

The Moon on the South Lake

Along the strip of land bordering the South Lake there was formerly only one state-operated factory, the Wuhan Third Pharmaceutical Factory. In recent years, protests of the city residents against pollution increased daily so that several chemical factories located in the densely populated areas were compelled to remove hither one after another. The place was becoming a chemical industry centre. On the eastern side of the zigzag asphalted road, a series of signboards pointed out to passers-by the location of these factories: the Central-South Chemical Factory, the Red Flag Chemical Factory, the Spark Chemical Factory, etc. Their names were all quite imposing and pleasant, but in reality they were all neighbourhood workshops, commonly called 'street factories', with only a hundred or so workers each. Some people looked down on them refusing even to call them factories, as if they were not worthy of such a designation. Nevertheless, they existed and expanded defiantly. Many of their products had no rivals throughout central and south China.

Take the Spark Chemical Factory for example. Its outer appearance was very poor. Nobody would speak well of it. But it turned out a wide variety of products, such as an anti-aging tincture, ferric chloride, ferrous chloride and also small rubber caps for soya-bean sauce bottles. Ferric chloride alone was indispensable as a water-purifying agent for the whole Wuhan Municipality. The full name of this small 'street factory' was the Spark Chemical Factory of Lion Street, Wuchang District, Wuhan Municipality, but on its official seal was engraved the Spark Chemical Factory of Wuchang District, Wuhan

Municipality, 'Lion Street' having been omitted. In order to omit these characters, the factory's Party secretary Wan had to do some explaining to her superiors. She said, 'The young men in our factory when courting their girls are worried that the words "street factory" will frighten them away. When they have some business to do, the other party on seeing the words "street factory" in the letter of introduction will treat them as inferiors.' These rather silly explanations, when uttered so seriously by Secretary Wan, seemed quite reasonable and convincing. In view of the important question of the young workers' marriages and of course also the more important one of the future of the factory, the authorities concerned, being reasonable, gave their tacit consent. But, although the status of the factory as shown on its official seal was thus noticeably elevated, what good had actually accrued? Whenever the factory wanted to buy some badly needed material, it still had to implore others for it, as if asking for a favour.[1]

Wasn't it so? Then, the fifty-year-old woman secretary was confronted with another difficulty. The factory's principal source of profit, ferric chloride, had to be changed from a liquid into a solid product. A three-story workshop had been built; all the necessary equipment was installed, save a boiler. In the words of Secretary Wan, 'The fire is singeing our eyebrows.' It was a desperate situation.

Speaking about Secretary Wan, it isn't wrong to regard her as a Party cadre, but it is also quite correct to look upon her as a housewife. Her ways and methods of work were all theoretically inexplicable, but in practice you had to do as she bid. When the factory needed something, she would strike the 'bell' (a piece of steel, two-feet long) summoning all the workers, and put the problem before them, asking them to suggest a solution. Then the fathers, brothers and sisters would go home to ask their families or call upon relatives and friends, or go by a still more roundabout way to ask acquaintances in certain organizations or larger factories to help. After a verbal

1. Capital goods were distributed by the government and could not be obtained on the market.

understanding had been obtained, a formal letter of introduction was written. Secretary Wan would herself make several visits. But this time, though the 'bell' had been struck and all relatives and friends had been importuned, no boiler had appeared. Finally, they heard some important information. The Jiangnan New Waterworks had recently purchased a large boiler. Their original smaller one was sitting in the courtyard of their living quarters. Two small factories had already made overtures. But the waterworks people said that they didn't want to give away the boiler, because they still needed it. Then they learnt that if only Assistant Manager Yuan, who was in charge of supplies at the said waterworks, would agree to sign an order, the boiler could be obtained with or without a letter of introduction. The strategy was mapped out. But no one dared to accept the assignment. Those who were in the know revealed that Assistant Manager Yuan was not an easy man to approach.

Dong, dong, dong . . . Secretary Wan again struck the steel bar. She asked if anyone was willing to go but no one responded. The workers remained looking at her.

'It's no use staring at me! What are we going to do?'

Suddenly a man in a low voice, 'Let me try!' Ordinarily no one would take any notice of this speaker. But now Secretary Wan and the workers were desperate. Whoever would accept the task was like a saviour to them. But when they saw clearly who the man was, they were all flabbergasted.

The volunteer was a young fellow named Ke Ting. With such a large crowd looking at him, his pale face at once turned a deep red. His tall frame, 1.85 metres, appeared especially striking.

'Well, you go and have a try. In any event . . . you must get it for me.' Secretary Wan looked at him nonchalantly with half-closed eyes. She had wanted to say. 'In any event, there is no one else available.' But as she stuttered she thought it best to give him a positive order.

Though Ke Ting held no position, he was a qualified technician, a jewel in the hands of Secretary Wan. The solid ferric chloride workshop which was soon to be put into operation was a large and somewhat modernized workshop. The blueprints and technological processes had all been worked out by him. Ke Ting had not studied in a technical college. The road he had travelled was the same as most Chinese urban youths: he had graduated from a senior middle school, been sent to the countryside for two years and after being brought back again entered a street factory. He had had no other choice. Soon he was able to solve the factory's multifarious technical problems. Whenever some new technology was to be adopted, you could rely on him. He would study the directions carefully, and make repeated experiments. He never let his colleagues down. The young men admired him and even the old workers regarded him as an unusual person. His main problem was that he was too shy. He had many fluent phrases in his mind, but when it came to speaking, the words choked him. No wonder that the older workers were surprised when such a shy young man, who had never before done any diplomatic work for the factory, now offered to obtain the required boiler.

Even Ke Ting himself doubted whether he would succeed.

2

In the flourishing shopping centre of Wuchang, two rather attractive girls could sometimes be seen, dressed alike, with similar bobbed hair, and about the same height, 1.72 metres. No matter how busy the streets, how many the pedestrians on the pavements, they would walk together, arm in arm. Because of their tall, neat figures, they attracted people's attention. Even arrogant youths had to make way for them, looking up at them while allowing them to pass. One of the girls had a round face. She was called Li Lu. The other with an oval one was named Yuan Xia. Schoolmates in different grades, their similar builds, inclinations and interests drew them together. They always had a lot to talk about. In their love affairs, they acted as each other's adviser. Their fundamental requirement was: the man should not be less than 1.85 metres tall. Good heavens! At present, when the percentage of tall people among the total population is not too high, it is not easy to find a young man 1.85 metres tall of about the same age residing in the same city, even if no other additional conditions such as family status, occupation and wages are taken into consideration. Whoever was the adviser had a hundred percent vetoing power. All decisions of parents and matchmakers were to no avail. For example, if anyone introduced a boyfriend to Li Lu, Yuan Xia would take a look at him. Her dignified nose would wrinkle in disgust, as she pronounced, 'An ugly dwarf!' Then Li Lu's expression would at once change; the affair was at an end.

The girls frequently went out together—that was until half a year ago. Then Li Lu found a boyfriend, approved by Yuan Xia. On Fridays, their day off, Yuan Xia would no longer figure in Li Lu's life so much. When Li Lu arranged with her boyfriend to visit Yuan Xia, the latter felt somehow that they were showing her consideration. Then she accompanied them back home. The sight of them cycling side by side like two riders on fine steeds on a grassland was quite enchanting. Yuan Xia's mother advised her to moderate her fundamental requirement: consider a boyfriend who was actually of the same height as her, or even slightly shorter. But this suggestion met with strong opposition both from Yuan Xia and Li Lu. Yuan Xia's mother said, 'Look at your father. He's shorter than me, but I have never found fault with him.' Yuan Xia eyed her coldly, saying, 'You want everybody to be like you!' Yuan Xia then summed up her requirements for a husband in a single phrase: a tall, honest, young man. And she openly announced this in her home.

Yuan Xia was a worker in the state-operated Third Pharmaceutical Factory, biking there every day. On a fine spring day in March, she thought of calling upon Li Lu on her way home to have a heart-to-heart talk with her. The road lay along an embankment of the South Lake. The evening sun was shining obliquely on the lake, producing many golden ripples. A circular range of green mountains was reflected on its surface. Yuan Xia now and then glanced at the scene, while she complacently rode past several 'ugly dwarfs'. To her surprise, a rider on a 'Phoenix 12' bicycle swept past her. She chased after him and taking advantage of his unawareness got ahead again. Looking back, she found that the cyclist was a tall fellow, of about the same height as Li Lu's boyfriend. That was interesting. After riding a little farther, she looked back again to find out if he had caught up. This in a way was an insult to the man, who was none other than Ke Ting returning home after work. We have learned that he was a modest fellow. But a modest person sometimes also behaves in a peculiar manner. When he realized that the girl was challenging him, he quickly passed her again. But Yuan Xia was not to be outdone. Using all her energy, bending both her arms backwards and flattening her body almost parallel to the ground, like an athlete she again brazenly sped ahead of Ke Ting. Without having time to straighten up, she suddenly heard a clanking noise and the pedals no longer worked. She glided on scores of metres more till her bike stopped. With her feet on the ground, her eyes wide open in astonishment, she saw Ke Ting ride past her. The 'ugly dwarfs' behind caught up and passed her, talking and laughing loudly at her, gloating over her discomfiture.

On hearing their laughter, Ke Ting looked back and saw the unhappy girl. He felt pity for her. Turning back, he described a half circle with the bicycle and stopped beside her.

'Let me have a look,' he said, taking out a small screw-driver and a small spanner and starting to fix the bicycle without waiting for the girl's permission.

He then tried the pedals and found the chain broken.

Helplessly, Yuan Xia stared at the young man and her bicycle and exclaimed, 'What a mess!'

Night was descending. The water in the South Lake changed from green to light blue, and then to bluish black. Both the lake water and the sky became unfathomable and mysterious. A chill gust of evening wind blew across the lake. Although Yuan Xia was 1.72 metres tall, she was after all a girl. In the company of a stranger and in this quiet place, she could not help feeling uneasy.

Slowly the moon rose, a bright and full moon. It silently lifted the veil on the South Lake. In the quiet spring night, only the moon and scattered street lamps shone on the young man and girl who had met by chance. Yuan Xia was worried about her bicycle and was also a little scared. Her heart was full of gratitude to Ke Ting. She wondered how to thank him. Then she reflected, she ought not to involve others in her trouble. But what would she do if he went away? Push her bike or carry it home? If he was going to leave . . . After considering the question, she decided that she had no alternative but to rely on this youthful stranger, who was now working hard to repair her bicycle and whose name she did not know.

'Look, let's do it like this,' Ke Ting said. 'If you will trust me, you can go ahead on my bike. Then your family won't feel so worried about you. I can repair your bike, but it still will take some time. Tomorrow we can exchange our bikes.' He decided to wheel the girl's bike back home if he could not repair it on the spot.

'But I don't like leaving you alone here,' Yuan Xia said sincerely.

'It seems you still don't trust me. You're afraid that I'll steal your bike! Don't worry. You have my licence plate. You can go to the police and easily find out my name and address.'

'No, I didn't mean that,' the girl hurried to explain.

'Then why stay here? I'll get up earlier tomorrow and bring your bike to the gate of your unit. Are you from the Central China Agricultural College or the Third Pharmaceutical Factory?'

The girl replied that she was from the latter, but still lingered there. She could not tell why. Ke Ting, however, repeatedly urged her to go, until she was convinced that there was really no need for her to stay. Then she rode away on his bicycle, her mind in a whirl.

Early the next morning, Ke Ting arrived and waited in front of the gate of the pharmaceutical factory. The exchange ceremony was very simple. It consisted of only two sentences. The one party asked in joyful surprise, 'You've fixed it?' The other replied factually, 'Yes.' Yuan Xia was full of gratitude and was wondering how to reward him. She was about to ask his name and address but the young man smiled, mounted his bike and rode away. Yuan Xia ran after him several steps and called out loudly, 'If you need my help, you can find me at the New Waterworks' living quarters.'

Yuan Xia's adviser Li Lu, having heard the above romantic story, slapped the table and exclaimed in surprise. She, however, criticized Yuan Xia for being slow. If she had taken down his licence number she could find out his name and then who knows what might result?

Yuan Xia defended herself, 'If you had been in my shoes, you'd have been as careless!' Though she said this, she actually felt regretful.

3

All practical Chinese citizens are well conversant with the ways of the world. In everything, people must depend upon each other for help. 'To help one another' is a master-key to open the doors of all locked offices. Ke Ting had helped Yuan Xia by repairing her bicycle, but he had never imagined that he might need the help of this girl stranger. Nor had he any ulterior motive in helping her. It was only when Secretary Wan mentioned the boiler in the New Waterworks' living quarters that he recollected what the girl had said to him.

On coming off duty, he rode directly to the New Waterworks' living quarters. In the courtyard he saw three blocks of flats and some old bungalows. Who was he looking for? Ke Ting felt nonplussed. He had not asked her name, so how could he ask for a certain girl whose bicycle had broken down on the embankment of the South Lake on a certain day? He suddenly became aware that his offer to Secretary Wan to try to obtain the boiler was a wild-goose chase. He scanned every window, hoping to see the face he still faintly remembered. When it grew dark, he could only leave the place in dejection.

The next day, when Secretary Wan saw him she asked, 'Young Ke, where's that boiler you were going to get?'

'I tried, but I failed,' he replied.

She asked again, 'Who were you looking for?'

'I didn't see anybody.'

Secretary Wan became impatient. 'Then go and look again!' she said. 'Who did you ask for? Maybe I can give you a tip. If you don't know what to say, I'll teach you.'

Ke Ting dared not tell her the truth. He could only say, 'I'll go and try again when my shift is over.'

Finding him still speaking of 'trying', Secretary Wan became even more exasperated. 'This isn't a joking matter! If you have any difficulty or if you must take a gift, tell me and I'll back you up. For one thing, you must take a packet of cigarettes with you.'

'Leave me alone! That person . . . doesn't smoke!'

We don't know how Secretary Wan was able to discover that the person Ke Ting was referring to was a young woman; perhaps she had noticed his expression and his hesitation. She laughed, no longer worried.

'You young fellow, can you kid me? I'll support you when you are courting. Talk about love and the boiler together! You can ask her to help you.'

Ke Ting said seriously, 'Secretary Wan, you shouldn't make fun of me.'

Displeased she asked, 'And why not?'

Without waiting for her to finish, Ke Ting ran away in embarrassment. He worked silently that whole day, left half an hour earlier and went to wait outside the gate of the pharmaceutical factory.

Its whistle sounded loudly. Ke Ting hurried to the bus stop and occupied a vantage-point. A host of well-trained cyclists emerged, gliding down the slope until they were some distance away. Ke Ting looked only at the female workers. He saw many of them, but not 'her'. He wondered if she was smartening herself up. Suddenly, she appeared, very neatly dressed, quite in accord with the time of year, yet not in the current fashion. She was pushing her 'Phoenix 18', surrounded by her girlfriends. Yes, it was her! Tall and slender, with an oval face and wheeling her bike, she was easily recognized. When she was at the factory gate, a moment's hesitation from Ke Ting critical moment, the young man's courage spurred him into crying out, 'Hello, Comrade!'

The girls saw a young stranger and smiled at each other, wondering which of them he was addressing.

Yuan Xia was surprised. She at once recognized him. Yes, it was he, whom she had thought of night and day, wanting to repay his kindness. 'Ah, young . . . Is it really you?' She was both surprised and happy, her face flushed.

Her companions all got off their bicycles. Looking at this tall couple, they all had the same thought. One of the girls made a wry face and called to Yuan Xia, 'Comrade Hello! Do you want us to wait for you?'

Of course, she didn't want them to wait! Yet Yuan Xia said, 'As you please.'

The girls' teasing, however, was not easily stopped. 'Be honest and tell us to beat it.' Then, they rode away quickly.

Ke Ting then said awkwardly to Yuan Xia, 'I've come to see you about something else.'

Such a declaration under such circumstances would hardly produce a good effect, yet the girl, finding him so embarrassed, giggled and said, 'Don't mind them, let's go that way.'

They mounted their bicycles and set off in the opposite direction to that taken by Yuan Xia's companions. They talked as they rode.

'I went to the New Waterworks' living quarters to find you.'

'When?'

'Yesterday, after I finished work.'

'I was at home. I didn't go anywhere.'

'There's so many apartment blocks.'

'My home is in the second building, second entrance, on the second floor. It's very easy to remember and find. Just ask for Yuan Xia. They all know me.'

This time, Yuan Xia's reply was quite positive and definite.

'Your father and mother are both old workers?'

'You can call father an old worker in the waterworks. Mother was formerly in a street factory. Later she was transferred to the waterworks.'

At the mention of a street factory, Ke Ting's most sensitive nerve was touched. This was why he was here. Feeling uncomfortable, he continued with some reluctance, 'Oh! Your father's an old worker. What's he in charge of?'

'Everything and nothing!' Yuan Xia replied mischievously.

Ke Ting caught on. 'You mean he's a cadre, not a worker.'

Now it was Yuan Xia's turn to feel discomfited. She countered, 'What if my father is a cadre? What if he is a worker?'

The girl's words were so sharp that the young man could only say honestly, 'I guessed you were from a cadre's family and your father is in a leading position. I didn't mean that an old worker could not be . . .'

On hearing this, Yuan Xia thought, 'You're like all the rest, a snob! When you were repairing my bike, you looked simple and sincere, but now you have become so vulgar . . .'

Displeased, she kept silent and rode on.

Realizing he had offended her, Ke Ting changed the topic and spoke to her about the boiler.

This dispelled her doubts. She laughed to herself to think that the young man certainly did not know after all that she was Assistant Manager Yuan's daughter. She then told him gently, 'Don't worry! Leave it to me!'

'Leave it to you? Are you sure? I heard that Assistant Manager Yuan isn't easy to talk to. Does your father know him well?

Annoyed and amused, the girl said, 'I told you to leave it to me. What more do you want?'

Ke Ting added, 'When it's all been fixed, I'll bring a letter of introduction.'

'Don't be so fussy! Let's talk about something else!' Yuan Xia looked with scorn at him. She felt that it was spoiling their fun to talk only shop.

4

After entering the living quarters of the New Waterworks, and rounding a corner, Ke Ting at once saw the desired boiler. He produced a steel tape to take its measurements. Yuan Xia became impatient and said, 'Even if the size of the boiler fits your needs, you don't know if they're going to give it to you.'

Ke Ting then hastily followed her into her home.

The place was easy to find. Ke Ting, however, was oblivious of his surroundings. He was still calculating in his mind the volume of steam the boiler could produce. The girl pushed open the door, grinned mischievously and announced, 'This is Assistant Manager Yuan's home.' The young man had not expected that she would take him directly to the discussion table, and felt very nervous. His heart sank. He asked doubtfully, 'Didn't you say that we would first talk it over with your father?' Yuan Xia said mysteriously like a skilled actress, 'It's all the same.'

Inside the small drawing room three or four people were shrouded in dense cigarette smoke. Their eyes swept over Yuan Xia and Ke Ting. Yuan Xia frowned, fanning the smoky air with her hand, pouting and exclaiming, 'Ugh!' She was tired of uninvited guests who frequently came to her home. A middle-aged guest rose to leave. He said, 'Manager Yuan, we'll do as you've suggested. When the time comes, I hope you will personally put in a good word for us.' The two others also rose and said, 'Manager Yuan, if you don't help us and put in a good word for us, our problem won't be solved. We'll have to come back and trouble you again.' Ke Ting had already taken a good look at Assistant Manager Yuan. He was a small man, not even of medium height, but his balding hair and shining forehead gave him a certain dignity.

When all the guests had left, Yuan Xia said to Ke Ting, 'You stay here and make yourself at home. I'll come back very soon.' Then she closed the door and went out.

With Yuan Xia gone, Ke Ting felt more uneasy. He didn't know what trick the girl was playing on him. Was it because Assistant Manager Yuan was so very hard to talk to that she had purposely left them after the first introductions?

'Assistant Manager Yuan—Manager Yuan, I'm sorry to trouble you . . .'

'No trouble at all! Sit down, let's talk it over.'

Assistant Manager Yuan took the tall young man brought by his daughter seriously. He smiled faintly and invited Ke Ting to sit down on the rattan chair beside the tea-table and poured out a cup of tea for him. Ke Ting felt that the manager was not as unapproachable as people said. Manager Yuan leaned against the desk in front of the window and the back of his chair and began to chat with the young man.

'You and Yuan Xia have known each other for a long time?'

'No.'

'How did you become acquainted?' Manager Yuan saw that the young man was clearly eligible as far as his height was concerned.

Ke Ting replied shyly and respectfully, 'It was by chance.'

The manager did not probe further. He picked up a small bottle on the desk, took out some pills and swallowed them with a little water. Then he ran his fingers through his hair and said benevolently, 'You didn't know each other before, but you're going to see more of each other from now on, understand each other better, eh?'

Ke Ting felt something was wrong; his face flushed and his heart beat rapidly. He remembered that when they talked about the boiler on their way there, the girl had insisted several times, 'Leave it to me!' And on entering the flat her manner was so easy, as if it were her own home. Could she be the daughter of Assistant Manager Yuan? Of course! She had the same surname. But when he looked at the small manager, he was again in doubt. However, he hoped that genetics might have played tricks in the present instance in favour of solving the problem of the required boiler. What luck if Yuan Xia was really the daughter of Assistant Manager Yuan!

However, he stuck to his prejudice regarding heredity. He cut short the manager's meditation and turned the subject of their talk to the business on hand. 'Manager Yuan,' he said, 'the problem is this. Our factory wants a boiler . . . the one in the courtyard. I've seen the brand and measured its size. It's exactly what we want. Yuan Xia brought me here. Will you please help us by agreeing?'

That did it! Till then Assistant Manager Yuan had been dreaming of being a father-in-law, but now he resumed the status of manger. He thought in disgust, 'More talk about that boiler!' So he kept silent for a long while.

Ke Ting begged, 'Our small factory needs your help, Manager Yuan.'

After a long pause the manager asked, 'What does your factory produce?'

'Our first product was called "anti-aging tincture".'

'"Anti-aging . . . tincture"? Ah! So you're making this! Is it really as good as it says?' The manager was quite interested. He toyed with the bottle of pills on his desk.

'It's not bad. Customers in other cities and the armed forces have placed orders with us.'

'Oh! That's proof enough. But I don't believe it can really prevent aging. I don't think it's really so effective.'

'It's been tested by the Chemical Research Institute. Our customers are also satisfied.'

The manager took up the bottle from the desk. 'How does it compare with these life-prolonging pills?'

'That's a different thing,' Ke Ting replied.

The manager laughed heartily. He held up his head, resting his weight on the two back legs of his chair and said, 'I think they're all the same. I've taken many bottles of these life-prolonging pills produced by Yuan Xia and her colleagues, yet I'm still going bald!' Then, as if to prove this, he again ran his fingers through his hair backwards. '"Life-prolonging pills", "anti-aging tincture", they're only pleasant names. At most, they'll do you no harm. Don't you agree?'

After a while, the manager sat up and his head and the chair legs again resumed the normal position. He said candidly, 'Now here's what we'll do. You go back and talk it over with your Party secretary and factory director to see whether you can supply us with some of your products while I can discuss your request with our other heads.'

Ke Ting knew then that the manager had mistaken the preparation to prevent the aging of rubber as a tonic to prolong life. He wanted to laugh, but dared not. He considered that if he told him the truth it would make the manager look a fool. So he could only say tactfully, 'So far we haven't sold it to any private customers, because its price is too high. Moreover, it can't . . .'

Manager Yuan, irritated by his roundabout reply, scowled and said, 'Yes, nowadays we all do everything according to the rules. Which factory is yours?'

The young man replied, 'The Spark Chemical Factory of Wuchang District.'

The manager looked puzzled. 'Has Wuchang District such a factory?'

Ke Ting replied, 'It's full name is "The Spark Chemical Factory of Lion Street, Wuchang District".'

'Oh, a street factory!' The manager didn't bother to hide his contempt. 'Now, we must act according to the rules. I'm not the only one in charge here . . . Isn't that right? Moreover, we may still need that boiler ourselves . . .' Anything else?'

This sounded like a dismissal. Ke Ting at once felt chilled and shivered as if he was ill. Humiliated, he regretted attempting to be a hero for his factory's sake.

'You're still young. Perhaps you haven't done much business before. From now on, you should bring a letter of introduction.' The manager stood up, a forced smile on his face.

This short man with his balding head! Ignorant! Foolish! Greedy! Snobbish!—Ke Ting almost spat the words out. He thought angrily, a street factory . . . So what? Haven't street factories made millions of dollars' worth of wealth for the country without asking the government for a cent? To tell the truth, he at first also had been prejudiced against them. He had studied on the side and secretly begged Secretary Wan to let him sit for the college entrance examinations, because that was the only way to get away from the street factory. Secretary Wan, however, had answered, 'The old workers treated you so well. Now that your wings are strong enough, you want to fly away. Aren't you sad to leave us?' With a sigh she continued, 'If you insist, I can't stop you. It would be selfish to consider only our interests and not those of the country as a whole. I wouldn't do anything to harm your future. But I hope you'll wait until I've found someone to replace you.' The young man's heart was offended; he wept, touched by her affectionate words. Emotions and his career were in conflict, and eventually the former proved victorious. He could not let down the old workers or Secretary Wan. He felt sorry for his leaders. Secretary Wan should have been at home taking care of her grandson, but instead she was up at half past four in the morning, taking three buses from north to south to get to work. Why was she so hard-working? The sixty-five-year-old factory director had to ride on a ramshackle bike a hundred-odd *li* back and forth each day in all sorts of weather. Why was he so hard on himself? Seeing Manager Yuan and comparing him with Secretary Wan and his factory director, Ke Ting appreciated them all the more. Their stature suddenly grew taller in his mind. They were so good, so affectionate to their workers!

Ke Ting rose as if he himself had become taller. In this small room, he had learned much, seen a microcosm of society with its multifarious strange phenomena. He wanted to ask, 'Mr Manager! Is that boiler your private property, or is it the property of the People's Republic of China?'

Ke Ting looked in disgust at the manager, and said the weightiest words he had ever uttered, 'Thank you, manager, for your instructions!' Then he turned on his heel and rushed out of the door.

He went down the forty steps, two at a time. He was opening the lock on his bicycle when someone caught his hand. He turned his head to look at a woman carrying a basket of food.

'Hey there! Why are you running away!'

Ke Ting was baffled.

'Look here, I've just bought some food. When Yuan Xia told me you'd come, I ran to the market as quickly as I could. Don't go yet, she'll come back very soon. She's been gone such a long time! Go up and sit a little more with her father.'

In this tall, warm-hearted, frank woman, Ke Ting easily recognized Yuan Xia. But he had been insulted, so he regarded her and her husband and also their daughter as the same; they were all making fun of him. He replied glibly, 'No, I haven't brought the required thing.'

Misunderstanding him, Mrs Yuan said hurriedly, 'What do you mean? What do you need to bring with you? I'm happy you came just as you are. You haven't had a bite and now you want to go. That won't do! Yuan Xia will blame me when she comes back. If you hadn't kindly helped her repair her bike, I really don't know what would have become of her that dark night.'

Ke Ting, however, freed his hand, saying, 'I'm too young and don't know anything. I didn't bring a letter of introduction!' He pushed his bike, got on and rode away.

Mrs Yuan gazed at his back and felt bad. This good young man had gone away! No doubt her old man must have offended him! Bring a letter of introduction! Such nauseating airs! He doesn't know whom he is talking to . . .

5

Yuan Xia had really gone on business—straight to Li Lu's home without having first called her on the phone. Learning that 'the man' had come, Li Lu was most curious to see her friend's hero. She therefore grabbed her bike and hurried off with Yuan Xia.

The two 'Phoenixes' flew side by side, the two girls talking and laughing merrily, leaving the street lights, trees, pedestrians and streams of traffic quickly behind them. It seemed that they were the tallest and happiest girls in the whole world. Good fortune was beckoning to them.

As was her wont, Li Lu gave a warning signal before she entered the flat. She called loudly, 'Uncle Yuan, Aunty Yuan, Li Lu has come again. Am I welcome?'

No one came out to welcome her, so she let herself in. *Aiya*! The small drawing-room revealed signs of battle. Father looked like a wounded captive, bending down his head awkwardly against the desk. Mother was standing before him full of fury.

Where was the young man? Gone?

Mother said angrily, 'Ask him!'

The manager begged for mercy. 'He helped us, so of course I'm going to help him! What more would you have me do?'

Mrs Yuan, now that reinforcements had arrived, launched a greater offensive, 'I don't care about your boiler, I want that young man!'

Her husband pleaded, 'Where can I find him for you?

Tomorrow you can ring up his street factory and say that I've agreed.'

Hearing the words street factory, Li Lu's heart sank. She wanted to ask Yuan Xia about it. She therefore tried to persuade Mrs Yuan to go and prepare the meal. Mrs Yuan, however, was not so easily pacified. Taking Li Lu by the hand, she abused the old man for his heartlessness, his disgusting airs. How could he ask for a letter of introduction? She declared she was not going to cook. She would rather 'let the old devil starve to death'. Her husband, fearing that their quarrel might arouse the girl, could only keep silent. Of the three, he was the shortest and the most unfortunate. Mrs Yuan did not stop abusing him until she was hoarse and exhausted.

As soon as she entered Yuan Xia's room, Li Lu asked, 'What's this? Your man's from a street factory?'

Yuan Xia replied reprovingly, 'Is a worker in a street factory less than a man, a second-class citizen?'

Li Lu chided, 'Oh! Don't get mad at me! I'm just afraid that your parents will object.'

Yuan Xia of course was not angry with Li Lu. She also did not think it necessary to explain this to her good friend. She said, 'My dear father with his iron rice-bowl has forgotten his begging bowl. If he had any respect for street factories, he would not have pulled every string to have my mother transferred to a state factory. When I hear others criticize bureaucracy and privilege, I feel glad and sad. Sad because I've been deprived of my right to make such criticisms.'

Then Yuan Xia continued that if a man had a good character, there was no need to fuss over certain disadvantages. Li Lu, out of a feeling of responsibility towards her friend, asked for particulars about the Spark Factory. Yuan Xia told her all that she knew and what Ke Ting had explained to her. She said that the ferric chloride produced by the Spark Factory was required by the Wuhan Steel and Iron Company in a big project with up-to-date imported equipment. A foreign specialist had suggested if they couldn't produce it, they could import it. But this small factory had produced it. Li Lu, finding Yuan Xia so fervent, could no longer dampen her ardour. The two girls quickly agreed on the 'fundamental requirement'. They then worked out a plan of action.

6

The next morning, Yuan Xia and Li Lu arrived very early at the Spark Chemical Factory. Of its appearance there was really nothing much to be said. Of course, if you looked at it from the viewpoint of struggling under difficulties, that was a different matter. Standing before the gate of the factory Li Lu could see everything at a glance. She remembered the numerous products, including the ferric chloride required for a modern steel plant that Yuan Xia had told her about the night before. She could only sigh, 'Who would have thought it!'

'He's come,' Yuan Xia whispered.

Li Lu looked up. The young man was pushing his bicycle up the sloping road in front of the factory. He was good-looking and tall. Her first impression was quite favourable. He wasn't inferior to her own boyfriend. Another exclamation, 'Who would have thought it!' She admired Yuan Xia's choice. Her round face became even rounder. She quietly urged Yuan Xia, 'Be more expressive, more active, more enthusiastic.'

Her three suggestions did not seem very effective. Yuan Xia had come to apologize, and also for some other purpose. She was usually an easy-going girl, but had now become rather tense.

Ke Ting had also changed, after having his baptism of fire in Manager Yuan's small drawing-room. His expression was cool, his eyes steady, like a crusader determined to fight all evil. He was surprised to see Yuan Xia. Why had she come with a companion? He tried to search for the harshest words, the most effective phrases to irritate her. He was going to ask her where she found the time to go slumming. Had she come to instruct him? If she wanted to purchase some anti-aging tincture so that her respected father could prolong his life, he would be only too happy to comply with her wishes.

'You've come very early,' Yuan Xia went forward to greet him.

'You . . . you're earlier than me,' Ke Ting stuttered. He was not used to fighting verbal battles. All the harsh and offensive words he had prepared in his mind vanished.

Silence followed. In international discussions, adjournments for several years are not unusual, but in talks between individuals a recess of a few seconds can be quite stifling. Silence is more terrible than open war.

Secretary Wan came along. She was chewing half a fried dough cake while walking. She called when she was still some distance away, 'Young Ke, have you got that boiler?'

'They want a letter of introduction!' Ke Ting aimed this at Yuan Xia rather than at the secretary.

'If you've made the arrangements, it's a simple thing to write a letter of introduction.' Secretary Wan, not aware of the circumstances, was evidently pleased. On coming nearer, she purposely sneezed and asked, 'Who are these two girls?'

Li Lu quickly piped up, 'Assistant Manager Yuan told us to come. Yesterday, after Comrade Ke had left, Assistant Manager Yuan said, "Don't let him come back and forth. We're all very busy with our work." So he personally wrote an order and told us to bring it here as soon as possible.'

Yuan Xia very much admired Li Lu's ability to gloss over her father's faults. She laughed up her sleeve. The fact was, the girls were afraid to allow the matter to stand for very long in case the boiler might be assigned elsewhere. Li Lu also wanted to see Yuan Xia's man herself so that she could better fulfil her responsibilities as an adviser. So they had compelled Manager Yuan to write the order himself.

Secretary Wan was full of gratitude. She wanted to drag the two girls to sit for a while in her office, but was afraid that her greasy hand might spoil their clothes. Li Lu, however, was more flexible and she followed her to her office. She told the secretary something of the events that had occurred. At the same time, she learned from the secretary some particulars about Ke Ting. The secretary was so pleased that she gazed for a long time with half closed eyes at Yuan Xia outside. Among their girl workers, some had married young workers of the pharmaceutical factory. Now, such a pretty girl from the pharmaceutical factory, and moreover, the daughter of Assistant Manager Yuan, had come over herself to their street factory. This certainly added much lustre to the secretary's face. She felt grateful to Assistant Manager Yuan for his generosity: he had not only given the factory a boiler, but had added a pretty young daughter into the bargain! 'Don't look down upon our small street factory. Assistant Manager Yuan himself has a good opinion of us!' she thought to herself with a sigh of satisfaction.

Yuan Xia apologized to Ke Ting. We must say that her attitude was quite sincere, and her self-criticism was thorough. Ke Ting was still in a bad mood. He didn't say anything. The 'bell' sounded again. He had to start work. Yuan Xia did not know whether or not he had forgiven her.

At dusk that day, on the embankment of the South Lake, in the same place where Ke Ting had repaired her 'Phoenix 18', Yuan Xia saw many bicycles pass quickly by. She wondered sorrowfully: Would Ke Ting keep his appointment with her? Or would he avoid her by taking a roundabout route? He ought to distinguish her from her father . . .

Translated by Hu Zhihui

Li Huiwen

A Manchurian writer born in Liaoning province in 1902, Li Huiwen had little formal education—one year of secondary school only—but had developed a knowledge of popular artistic forms from his father who was a shadow-show puppeteer. From the time he first learned to write in primary school, he was often called upon to copy out the scripts for the shadow-play programmes. Like a number of the other writers whose work we have selected, he thus had an early involvement with popular tales and developed an interest and a talent for literary work, despite his lack of early formal training. This was to be fostered in later life. After his one year in secondary school it was necessary for him to learn a trade. In the fifties he returned to his region to work as a farm worker and a labourer. He began to write in 1958. He has produced several collections of short stories, among them *Chess for Three* and *Partings and Reunions*. He has also written a satirical novel.

His short story, *Biography of a Wild Man,* won a prize as a superior work in the competition held in 1981 for excellent stories by ethnic minority writers. *The Poster* is from the *Chess for Three* collection and outlines in a satirical way some of the difficulties that peasants, who were used to getting by as individual families, had in adapting to the collective way of life.

Li Huiwen

A Poster

Wang Baoman hitched the production team's ox to a small cart, in order to fetch his married daughter. Days before, the team's management committee had put up a poster praising him, which he wanted to show to her.

His face, with a few freckles dotting his nose, always wore a sheepish, unfathomable smile. He knew his daughter regarded him as a good-for-nothing. Whenever his name was mentioned, the villagers shook their heads, remarking, 'Don't talk to him. He's so selfish.'

It was no exaggeration. He tried to profit from every situation. Once, before he sold a pig to the team, he stuffed it with food to make it a lot heavier. No wonder Chunlan, his daughter, said, 'He's never done anything good for the collective.'

But the old man, used to this, thought contentedly, 'No matter what you think of me, my girl, you still have to call me father.'

But recently he had done something good. One day the team leader had found him angrily driving a pig away from the vegetable patch. This was so unusual that he asked the accountant to write a poster to praise the old man. Unable to find a large piece of paper the accountant took down an old notice about forest protection from the wall outside and wrote on the back of it with a brush. Then he put it up in the same place. The news soon got around. When the villagers met the old man they said, 'Congratulations, Uncle Wang!' Or 'Now you've got something to boast about!'

Wang felt greatly honoured. Nothing like this had ever

happened before. His head began to swell. 'I didn't do much,' he thought, 'but they praise me a lot. If I really did something great they might parade me about in a sedan-chair.' Yet at the same time he felt ashamed of himself. It was all a misunderstanding, though fortunately no one really knew what had happened. Anyway, the poster did him a great deal of credit, making up a lot for the past errors. If his daughter knew about it, she would not call him selfish and backward any more. This was why he had decided to bring her home for a visit.

Back home, he whispered to his wife in a conspiratorial way, 'What a stroke of luck! This morning a pig was on our private plot, so I chased it off. It ran away through the team's vegetable field. Just then, the team leader happened to see me and thought I was protecting the team's field. They're praising me highly for it.'

'How?'

'They've put up a big poster!'

'A big poster?' She was taken aback.

But why was she so shocked?

2

The word 'poster' meant trouble to her. She reckoned her husband must have done something wrong. Praising him? Impossible! Even if there was a poster how could he know what it was about? He couldn't read. He must be mistaken! The more she thought about it, the more worried she became. Memories from the past flooded her mind . . .

One autumn, her daughter, who was then not married, quarrelled violently with her father. It all started over the team's notice about harvest protection. Wang knew the effect of such a notice. Thinking his private plot was rather far away for him to keep an eye on, he wanted to put up a similar notice on the tree near his plot to scare off would-be intruders. This notice was outside the committee's office. After racking his brains for a while, he hit on the idea of removing the notice. If questioned later, he would say a notice at the roadside attracted more people. Naturally people would think he meant well. When no one was looking he took it off the wall. Unfortunately, unable to read, he took by mistake a notice about enrolment instead. The next day this notice attracted quite a crowd of youngsters who stood in the shade reading it and chewing maize stalks. What's more, it also drew many small kids who ran and played around the willow tree. The result was that some of Wang's crops as well as those of the team were damaged. Hearing about this, the leader determined to find out who had removed the notice. Chunlan, a member of the team's management committee, guessed that it must have been her father. So at the committee meeting, she mentioned this.

When she got home, she tried to sound out her father, 'Father, somebody's done us a good turn.'

Puzzled, Wang asked, 'What?'

'Someone has put up a notice on the willow tree near our plot.'

'Oh,' he said, slowly lowering his head. 'That's good! Near the road everybody can see it.'

'But it's the wrong place for an enrolment notice. Now children are running about, eating the maize stalks. The crops are being damaged!'

'What?' Wang looked up. 'Ours too?'

'What do you think?'

At this, Wang's wife began to curse, 'Who would play such a mean trick? Why put up a notice near our plot of all places?'

'Mind your tongue,' Wang reproached her. 'Probably he meant well.'

'Meant well?' Chunlan could do longer check her anger. 'Let's not beat about the bush, father. You've done a very stupid thing!'

'What do you mean?' he asked, trying to be calm and pretending to know nothing about it. 'You're always picking on me,' he complained. 'Did you see me do it? It's so unfair. Now our own crops are damaged. Who can I complain to?'

'You did it, so go and complain to yourself!'

'Stop answering back! Dammit!' Wang exploded. 'Everybody shows me more respect than you. To hell with you!' He slammed the door and left.

The talk soon died down, but not before everybody in the village had heard it.

Chunlan soon got married and moved to live in Phoenix Village, fifteen *li* away. With one thorn less in his flesh, Wang became bolder. Whenever he had the chance, he went and chopped down the team's trees. When he had gathered quite a pile of logs, he stored the wood in his home. One day his daughter came for a visit and discovered this. She wanted to report it at once to the team's management committee.

'Chunlan,' her mother pleaded, 'you're no longer a girl or a cadre. Don't meddle in your father's affairs. His disgrace won't do you any good.'

'Do you think I quarrel with him for my own good?' she said calmly.

'For what then?'

'If I only thought of myself, I wouldn't bother with him. I wouldn't have interfered in anything he did wrong. But every time he does something wrong and I argue with him, it's for his own good.'

'That's not to your credit. You should be ashamed to mention those quarrels!' Her reproachful, yet affectionate tone made Chunlan giggle.

As they were chatting, Wang entered. Since Chunlan was back, he was worried lest she discover his secret. But he was quite unprepared for her sudden thrust, 'Father, where did you get all those logs from?'

'Well . . .' He turned pale immediately. Rubbing his unshaven chin to hide his embarrassment, he said, 'They're somebody else's.'

'Whose?'

'Oh, several people's. It's none of your business!'

'Why shouldn't I ask?' Chunlan became determined. 'Those are the poplars we women planted. I've a right to ask.'

For a moment Wang said nothing. But he thought, 'I've married you off. You're not to interfere in my affairs any more. If you're going to be difficult, I'll send you packing!'

His daughter would not let the matter rest. Wang lost his

temper. As he was about to yell, Chunlan said, 'Haven't you seen the government notice about forest protection?'

At this, his anger cooled instantly. A government notice was not something to trifle with.

'Where is it?' he asked with apprehension.

'When I came here yesterday I saw the team leader pasting it on the wall outside the committee's office.'

'What does it say? I haven't been told about it yet.'

'Everybody is responsible for protecting publicly-owned trees. Whoever fells them without permission is breaking the law.'

This sent a shiver down the old man's spine. Shaking, her mother pleaded in a trembling voice, 'Oh! We'll really get into trouble now. Don't tell anyone, Chunlan, please!' Then she turned to her husband and said, 'Now you've got yourself in a mess, you old fool! Didn't I tell you not to do it? But no, you wouldn't listen to me. Now, you'll just have to lump it!' In exasperation, she vented her anger and let the cat out of the bag.

Now Wang was in agonies, knowing that his daughter would not let him off. What was to be done? He thought of trying to talk her round and begging her to forgive him just that once.

But before he could speak, Chunlan asked, 'It's as clear as day, father. What will you do now?'

'You won't take me to court, will you? I promise not to do it again. All right?' said the old man, crestfallen.

'That won't do. You must go to the management committee and confess and return all the logs.'

Since she had been a cadre, Wang knew that she was aware of the law. But he was too scared to go.

'So you're not willing to mend your ways? OK, I'll go instead of you.'

After this, Wang said hurriedly, 'All right! All right! I'll go now.'

In the committee's office, he made a clean breast of what he had done to the team leader. To his surprise, the man praised him for his good attitude. All Wang was asked to do was to make a self-criticism before the villagers. There would be no punishment. The old peasant insisted, however, that he would not be able to utter a word in front of so many people.

'Well, you can ask somebody to help you write a self-criticism.'

Back home, he repeated to Chunlan what the leader had said. His daughter found a large piece of paper and started writing. Then she read it over to him and he nodded approvingly. He went and pasted it on the wall outside the committee's office. But to himself, he thought, 'How disgraceful! My name on a poster!'

As promised, he behaved quite well afterwards and never did anything to harm the collective interest. Now he was being praised for driving a pig out of the team's vegetable field. There was a poster praising him in the same place where he had once put up his self-criticism. What a great pity if his daughter did not see this. Not caring what his wife thought, he decided to fetch his daughter.

3

As he was busy hitching up the ox to the cart, the stockman asked him to oil the wheels and muzzle the ox so as to prevent it from eating the crops. He complied. In high spirits, he set off. When he passed the poster, he had a close look at it to make sure it was still there, intact. Reassured, he drove the ox-cart out of the village.

There was a vast expanse of green crops. Sorghum and corn would soon be sprouting. Tender, lush, dewy leaves gleamed in the morning sun. The promise of a good harvest gladdened his heart. To be frank, he rarely had such feelings towards the team's crops. Perhaps the poster had elicited them. 'The crops will ripen soon,' he thought. 'There should be a notice to ask people to protect them.' Suddenly he caught sight of some kids, each chewing on a maize stalk. Wang halted and jumped off the cart.

'Hey! What do you think you're doing?' he bellowed. 'You'll damage the crops!'

'They're not yours. Mind your own business!'

'What! They're the team's. You call that none of my business? What cheek! Put them down! If the management committee had put up a notice to warn you, I'd have punished you for what you're doing.'

Some were scared and threw the stalks on to the roadway. But one retorted boldly, 'If there had been one, you'd have torn it down, wouldn't you?'

Wang flew into a rage. 'Dammit! You little bastard! Just wait till I get my hands on you!'

The boy made a face at him and ran away. Wang removed the ox's muzzle and fed it with all the stalks the children had left on the ground.

'You old meany!' the children protested. 'You've taken away our stalks to give to your own ox!'

'Are you blind? Is this my ox?' he snapped.

He produced a tobacco pouch, filled his pipe and began to smoke, waiting for the ox to finish eating. Then muzzling it again, he continued on his way.

Having threaded through the sorghum and millet fields, he guessed that he was now beyond his team's boundary. Taking the muzzle off the ox again, he let it chew the crops at random.

Suddenly a man emerged from a millet field. Wang recognized at once that he was from his own village and must be guarding the crops.

'Listen,' he said, 'you'd better keep your eyes skinned for those damned brats. I just caught a gang of them picking maize. Our committee ought to have put up a notice about it.'

Hearing 'notice', the man laughed and said, 'Yes. Where are you going?'

'To bring my daughter back home for a visit.' She should rest for a few days with her mother before the harvest starts.

'Well, you've forgotten to muzzle your ox.'

'No. Here it is.' Waving the muzzle, he explained, 'I just took it off.'

'Just took it off? But it'll eat the crops, won't it?'

'But surely those aren't our fields, are they?'

'That doesn't matter.'

Wang was silent, his face darkened. He thought, 'Can't you see it's our team's ox? What's wrong with a free feed? Aren't you one of us?'

Phoenix Village was not very far. When he got there, however, it was almost noon, for the ox moved very slowly. His daughter lived at the end of the big village. He first had to skirt round a temple to get there. As he passed it he spotted an eyecatching notice on its wall. It had just been put up, and the paste had not yet dried. One corner fluttered in the wind. Wang recognized an old man who was reading it as Chunlan's uncle-in-law.

'What does it say?' he jumped off the cart, asking.

'Oh, it's you! Our team has put up a notice here about our crop protection. Are you coming to fetch your daughter?'

'Yes.' Wang chuckled, admiring the team's vigilance, 'they are really on their toes putting up such a notice,' he said to himself. 'I must suggest it to our team leader.'

4

Seeing her father in the ox-cart, Chunlan went to meet him. She looked slim in her light blue blouse, black trousers, white socks and black cloth shoes. While wiping her hands on her apron, the rosy-cheeked girl sized up her father with her large shining eyes. He was a picture of joy. There was no sign of his usual sheepish smile, nor the desperate frown on his forehead.

She helped her father unhitch the ox and brought some fodder for it. She had just given birth to a son a month before, so she guessed that her parents wanted her to go back and stay with them for a while. But why was her father so smug? He was capable of anything. It was true he had been taught a lesson, but had he really turned over a new leaf? She doubted it.

Inviting him into the house, she offered him some tobacco. While filling his pipe, he pointed to the baby on the bed and asked, 'Where's his father?'

'Guarding the crops. He's at it all day long.'

'Where's his grandpa?'

'The same. He's so concerned about the collective. He's

often cited as a model peasant.' Chunlan emphasized this on purpose.

But Wang thought, 'That's nothing compared with the poster praising me.' He drew on his pipe and asked, 'How's your private plot?'

'Doing all right. What about your team?'

'Oh, it's not bad either.'

Puffing at his pipe, he thought hard to find an excuse to ask her to go home with him. It would soon be harvest time, and she would not easily be pursuaded.

'Your mother's sick,' he lied. 'We need your help.'

'Really?' Chunlan was surprised. She was a little suspicious, but he had come in the team's ox-cart. He would not have been lent it unless her mother was seriously ill. She decided to go back with her father.

After lunch, they set off, the baby in Chunlan's arms. As the ox plodded past the temple, Wang saw the notice on the wall again. He was thinking how to tell his own team leader, when a gust of wind blew the notice off the wall on to the ground. Glancing at Chunlan to see if she had noticed it, he saw she had not. Then it suddenly occurred to him, since there was no one about, to pick it up and take it to his village where he could paste it up. The committee might even write another poster praising him and let Chunlan know what a good fellow her father was. Beware anyone who would dare to call him selfish in future!

As the ox-cart turned the bend, he jumped off, saying, 'I must go and pee. I shan't be long.' He went back to the wall and, looking around, picked up the notice, which he folded and stuffed into his shirt.

The father and the daughter said little on the way. As they entered their village, the sun was setting. Near the committee's office, the old man began to fidget, in expectation of his daughter's happiness in reading the poster. 'Let's see what you'll say to that,' he thought. When they reached the poster, he stopped the ox-cart and asked, 'What's that on the wall, Chunlan?'

She replied after a glance, 'A notice, of course!'

'I know. But what's it about?'

Chunlan looked at it a second time. Unbelievable! A poster full of praises for her father!

'Father!' she cried out emotionally, tears dancing in her eyes.

Seeing his daughter's joy, he impulsively reached to produce the other notice from his shirt, but then he thought better of it.

When they got home, Chunlan found her mother lying in bed. What a shock Wang got to see his wife was really ill. 'But she was well this morning,' he wondered. 'What happened?'

5

His wife's illness was caused by her anxiety and fears. She had no idea what the poster was about. Then since her husband had been in such a great hurry to fetch his daughter she felt sure he must have got into deep trouble and was hoping Chunlan would put in a good word for him.

Chunlan decided to stay for a few days to care for her mother.

But three days later, her brother-in-law came with a donkey to take her back as her husband had fallen ill too.

'What's the matter?' she asked.

'Some of our crops have been damaged recently. My brother was overworking and so he fell ill.'

'But we put up a notice about our crop protection!'

'Damn it!' the young man said shaking his head. 'We're trying to find the rat who took it away!'

Wang, standing beside them, was shocked.

Just at that moment, the team leader entered laughing. 'Old Wang,' he said. 'how come you put up a notice belonging to Phoenix Village in our village? I couldn't believe it when someone told me. Then I went to see for myself and it really was true. You'd better send it back there.' So saying, he put the notice into Wang's hand and left.

The old man blushed to the roots of his hair.

Chunlan looked away, deeply embarrassed. She was happy when her father made even a little progress, but this was ridiculous and irritating!

'What's all this about, father?' she demanded.

Hanging his head, Wang said remorsefully, 'You know. Don't rub it in please.'

'What will you do then?'

'Now don't make a fuss, Chunlan,' her mother interjected from her bed. 'You'd better take it back and put it up again without anyone knowing. You mustn't let your father lose face in your village. It won't bring you any credit.'

'All you think of is saving face, but that doesn't seem to bother him!'

'You old fool!' Wang's wife cursed her husband. 'What a mess you've gone and got yourself into!'

Silent for some time, Wang suddenly slapped his thigh and said, 'All right, Chunlan. Say no more. I'll make a clean breast of it. Get a large piece of paper and write another self-criticism for me. I'll apologize to the people of Phoenix Village. After all, I'm to blame.'

'In that case,' Chunlan said cheering up, 'you'll save your face.' Though she had had only six years of schooling, her handwriting was fairly good. Before long, she had finished and read it over to him.

Wang, his head still low, exhaled a long trail of smoke as if blowing away his selfishness. He then removed the pipe and said, 'It's not enough just admitting my mistakes. Better add: I promise not to do such a thing again.'

'Yes, father. I know what you mean.' Chunlan smiled.

November 1962

Translated by Wang Mingjie

Poems

Ai Qing

Ai Qing's experiences are particularly pertinent to modern poetry in China since he writes within the social system but has strong, unshakeable convictions of what poetry is and has been determined to canvass those convictions in the course of his long working life. His age is relevant too; his career began in the early-thirties and encompasses the hey-day of the early Marxist writers, the first years of the Communist state and the Hundred Flowers and its aftermath—the 'anti-Rightist campaign'. Then there were twenty-odd years of literary silence until 1977 when once more he took up his pen to write for an audience other than himself. In an interview with this writer,[1] he remarked wryly that it was about time he started writing again because they said to him that if he didn't write something people would start to say he was in league with the Gang of Four.

Ai Qing is known for his poems as early as the thirties as the

1. The writer spent a morning interviewing Ai Qing and his wife Gao Ying, at their home in Beijing in August 1980, while working for a Ph.D thesis. The interview was recorded on tape.

poet of the North China prairies and the downtrodden peasants of the North. His poems on these subjects—*North China, The Handcart, Beggars*—are to be found in some early collections of modern Chinese poetry[2], as are his stirring war lyrics written during the period of the Japanese occupation of China—*The Trumpeter, He Died a Second time, Snow has fallen on the Chinese Earth*.

Although he wrote of the North, Ai Qing was born in South China. He was the rejected son of a Zhejiang landowner and initially studied art. He was part of the wave of young people who had work-study experience in France in the late twenties. He studied and painted in Montparnasse and worked at a pottery works. He came back to China in 1932, filled with revolutionary aspirations only to spend several years in detention in a Nationalist cell in Shanghai. His first published works were written there. *My Wetnurse—Dayanho, the Flute* and others.

After his release and some three years spent wandering in central and south-east China, he joined the Communists in Yanan.

Before the Yanan Forum on Literature and Art held in May 1942 Mao Zedong had several talks with Ai Qing during which they exchanged their views on various aspects of literature and the arts. There ensued the Yanan Forum on Literature and Art, which became the definitive statement that was to guide literary policy in China from then on, with brief periods of modification, the most recent of which is likely to be lasting.

He spoke out again in the Hundred Flowers period of 1956 in allegorical mode, with *The Cicada,* who sang only one song. This criticism of the increasingly monistic line in literature was seized on by his critics in the clampdown the following year. He was denounced as a Rightist and stigmatized as anti-Party. His punishment was virtual banishment, first briefly to the north-east and then to the Xinjiang in the west, where he, his second wife and family of four were later, during the Cultural

2. Kai-yu Hsü, *Twentieth Century Chinese Poetry;* Julia Lin, *Modern Chinese Poetry* and Robert Payne, *Twentieth Century Chinese Poetry*.

Revolution, to live in a Uighur dugout and engage in manual labour on the State farm.

These farms, which are set up in arid wilderness areas, provide the most arduous of living conditions, since they have to be built up from nothing. There are few amenities—minimal, if any, medical attention, for example—but Ai Qing did not complain of the length of his banishment or even the hard work, which at the height of the Cultural Revolution included the demeaning duty of cleaning out latrines. The local people were good to him and accepted his family into the community. There were others at the time, much worse off than himself. He still had his salary while many had to exist on a pittance based on what they themselves could produce with inexpert hands.

Poems of Ai Qing that are included in this collection have all been published since 1979 and so represent his latest creative phase. When asked what was the future for poetry in China, he refused to identify a likely mainstream: 'To say it will be *vers-libre* or folk-song or modern regulated verse, or even Tang style poetry is too much akin to reading oracles.' Nevertheless, his views are sanguine and he draws his optimism from the current healthy state of publishing in China, even of poetry journals, of which he gave the following résumé:

Each issue of *Poetry* (Shikan) has a circulation of one hundred and seventy thousand copies. As for *People's Literature* (Rénmin Wénxué), their print runs are about seven hundred thousand, not to mention all the new provincial publications.

The Wall

Like a knife, the wall
Slices the city into two
One half in the East,
One half in the West.

How high is the wall?
How thick?
How long?
No matter how high, how thick, how long
It couldn't be higher, thicker, longer
Than China's Great Wall.

Is it only a relic of history;
A wound of the race?
No one likes such walls.

Three metres high, so what!
Fifty centimetres thick, so what!
Forty-five kilometres long, so what!

Were it a thousand times higher,
A thousand times longer,
Still it could not block
The clouds in the sky, the wind, the rain, the sunlight.

Still it could not obstruct the birds' wings and the nightingale's
     song,
Still it could not hamper
The flow of air and water,
Still it could not hinder
A million people's thoughts, freer than the wind,
Their will more solid than the earth,
Their desires, more enduring than time.

The Mountain wind

The mountain wind is a sculptor;
Day and night, it scours
Year in, year out, it buffets.

Sometimes it wields cleaver and axe,
Rockfaces collapse like buildings.
Sometimes it whittles and buffs away,
Cuts the rocks into fragments,
Grinds them to powder, turns
Them to mud and sand.

When the snow and ice thaw,
   Mountain torrents rage;
Powder and mud alike
   Tumble together
   On their downward flow . . .

The wind
Is an assiduous sculptor.
Even late at night,
   It is loathe to rest.
Under its tenacious will,
Even the hills are transformed.

Spirits

She is lovely,
Has a personality all fire
In a fluid body.

She is the spirit of delight.
Where there is festivity
There she attends.

She really can tease,
Can make you speak the truth,
Draw out your heart.

She will make you
Forget your pain,
Delirious with joy.

Drink up, to victory
Drink up, to friendship
Drink up, to love

But you must take care,
when you are merry,
She'll steal away your reason.

Don't think she is water and
Can strike out your worries
She is oil, poured on fire.

She makes the bright ones brighter,
The dull ones more stupid.

Echo

She hides in the ravine;
She stands on the hillside.

You ignore her;
She ignores you.

You call her, she calls you;
You curse her, she curses you.

Whatever you do don't argue with her;
The last word is always hers.

Hope

The friend of dreams,
Sister to imagination.

She should be your shadow,
Yet she always precedes you.

Formless as light,
Restless as the wind.

She shares a room with you
But always keeps her distance.

Like a bird in flight,
Or a travelling cloud;

Like a butterfly by the lake,
Coquettish but beautiful.

You approach and she flies off,
You ignore her, she taunts you.

She will stay with you forever,
Until you take your last breath.

Monument to Death

Is this a vine trellis?
Is it a cane lattice?
Is it a heap of rusted metal,
A pile of junk?

No, it is none of these,
Please look at it closely.

These are corpses hanging on a barbed-wire
    fence;
Each one of them skin and bone,
They stretch out hands that cannot clench,
They scream despairing cries,
Defiant accusations.

Like a wailing steam-whistle
That shrills beneath the blue sky,
Shrills in every ear,
These sounds
Surmount this cache of time
To penetrate to future epochs
Forever and forever . . .

The Colosseum of Ancient Rome

Perhaps you have once seen
A spectacle such as this—

A small, round, clay pot,
Two crickets locked in battle
Each combatant rustles his wings,
Emits bursts of metallic sound
As he leaps at his opponent, jaws and
     arms working;
They charge and grapple.
After the long trial of strength,
One always comes out the stronger,
Tears off the other's leg,
Bites open his abdomen—relentless till his death.

The Colosseum of Ancient Rome
Was just like this.
Can't you imagine
The heroic scene:

Ancient Rome was the famous *City of Seven Hills*
East of the Palatine,
North of the Caelian,
South of the Aeschyline,
In the centre of the basin so formed
There is, perhaps
The world's largest amphitheatre.
It is like a round fortress;
From a distance, a four-storied edifice,
Each storey ringed with tall archways,
The circles inside are stands carved from stone;
It holds a hundred thousand spectators.
Visualize the day of the contest,

Probably a day of celebration,
It is more festive than a temple fair.
The Ancient Romans dress for the occasion
And converge on this place from everywhere,
Truly, mountains and seas of people.
The whole city is jubilant,
As though celebrating their victories in Asian and African
     campaigns;
In fact they have come to see a brutal tragedy,
To take their pleasure in another man's pain.

The trumpet sounds,
Death takes the ground.

The gladiators are all slaves,
Selected each one, for his bodily strength;
They are captives from defeated countries
Who've long ago lost wives and sons—their families ruined,
     themselves destroyed
And sent in chains to the Colosseum
to administer a death sentence that needed no proclamation.
They face a butchered end,
Like beasts in an animal pen.

The two who fight share no grievance or enmity,
Yet the same fate has been arranged for each
He must use a guiltless hand
To kill a blameless foe.
Each knows, he too must die,
Yet pins his hopes on the sharpness of his blade.

Sometimes they must fight wild animals,
A wild beast, well fed or starving, is always fearsome:
It craves warm, fresh blood.

If a slave at this point has courage,
It is born of despair;
For it's not intelligence that's needed here
But the strength to beat one's opponent.
See how arrogant those 'roughnecks' are,
They are the amphitheatre's hired hands.
Hulking, bull-necked brutes,
Holding iron clubs and leather whips,
(They start out wearing face-masks
Then even these, they discard),
They herd the gladiator out for the kill—
To undergo his death throes.
The blindfolded gladiators are the most piteous
(I wonder what idle mind
Devised such a cruel lurk!)
When in battle neither can see,
Each side slashes wildly with his sword seeking the enemy—
Attacking or defending, it is all done blindly—
They die blindly, win blindly.

One contest finishes;
The 'roughnecks' enter the arena.
With long-handled hooks they drag out the bodies
And the dripping pieces of flesh.
They drag to one side the men near to death,
Gather up weapons and other acoutrements
And kill those breathing their last;
Then bring water to wash away the dirty blood
So no trace of it remains.
These 'roughnecks' receive instructions from others;
Who don't kill directly,
Yet are more sinister than executioners.
Look again at the tiered stands,
So many thousands, frantic with pleasure.
Rank and station are clearly divided;
Seats allocated as befits position:
The Emperor and nobles languish luxuriously

Beside them their obsequious, fawning attendants.
Those courtesans, powdered and painted;
You might say, they have come to see the fights
But more truly they've come to display
Their youthful beauty;
Like stars from the heavens come to shine on the world of men.

There are the 'victors of many glorious campaigns', who live
In palaces built by slaves with their bare hands
And treacherous wives from vanquished countries,
Their eating utensils are stained with blood,
They savour the stench of blood.

The man, who can watch a man fight a beast
Must have something of the beast in him—
To derive enjoyment from the game of blood-letting,
To be able to laugh at the agonies of death.
The more others suffer, the happier such people are;
(Don't you hear the laughter?)
Most contemptible
Are those who capitalize on others' misfortune,
Who fish for profit in the pools of blood;
Their wealth grows apace with their crimes.

The more nervous the slaves in the arena,
The more excited the onlookers ranged around;
The louder the shouts of combat,
The more violent their shrieks of laughter.
Among the spectators, that is gilded headwear gleaming,
In the arena, those are swords and daggers glinting;
The two not far from one another,
Yet with an unassailable wall between.

This, then, is the Colosseum of Ancient Rome.
It lasted through so many centuries;
Who can tell how many slaves
Gave their lives in this round basin.

God, Zeus, Jupiter, Jehovah,
All the so-called 'Almighty gods' where were you?
Why did you remain aloof and indifferent to man's mis-
    fortunes?
Wind, rain and thunder,
How can you condone these crimes?

Slaves will always be slaves
But who was dominating mankind?
Who was the instigator of these games in the arena?
We see it more clearly, as time passes:
The operators of the Colosseum were the slave-owners
Whether it be old Tarquinius, or Sulla, Caesar, Octavion . . .
All were slave-owners among slave-owners—
Creatures with a bloodlust, tyrannical rulers!

'We must not be slaves!
We must be free men!'
One man calls
Ten thousand echo.
To change our fate
We must smash all evil amphitheatres;
Take those who gamble with other men's lives
And nail them to pillars of shame!

The slaves' leaders
Must be bred among slaves;
A common fate
Breeds similar thinking;
A common will
Meshes into a powerful force.
Raise again and again the righteous banner,
Only fighters can grow through defeat,
Angry troops like great waves of the Mediterranean
Submerge the palace, overturn the triumphal arch
Batter down the amphitheatre,
    a mighty horde

Of awakened people swear to water their land with fresh blood
To build a paradise of free labour.

Now, the Colosseum of Ancient Rome
Has become an historical legacy;
   like the ruins of war
Bathed in the last rays of the setting sun,
   like a fortress
It forces me to question and consider:
Is it, after all, a monument to glory
Or a symbol of shame?
Does it boast the splendour of Ancient Rome
Or attest to the barbarity of its rule?
Should it evoke cheap pity
Or strive for distant sighs?

Even the marble weeps,
After the abuse has gone on for too long;
Gone is this cruellest phase of the slave society,
The iniquitous slaughter has been lost in the mists of history
But has left a shameful memory in the conscience of mankind,
Has revealed a principle to us:
A debt of blood, will be repaid in blood;
Those who gamble with others' lives;
Will meet an ignoble end.
To say so, may seem somehow absurd—
Yet in the world, today
There are still those who preserve the slave-owner mentality.
They see the whole of mankind as candidates for slavery;
The world itself as a great Colosseum.

Burnt out

A tiny match
Marks out new boundaries—

Such a blaze
The wastes have become seas of fire!

Sparks dance and swirl,
A column of fire spurts to the heavens!

The flames like a golden doe
Race swifter than the wind.

Billowing smoke in the sunlight
Is like layers of gorgeous clouds.

The flames laugh wildly, run about
Blaze through all obstacles, delightedly.

The fire's troops make a bold advance,
Jackals, wolves, foxes and rabbits dodge out of their way.

If the fire does not burn out,
The grain shoots will not come up.

Quickly let us sharpen our ploughshares
And turn the first sod of a new age!

Translated by Christine Liao

Shu Ting

Shu Ting, now in her early thirties, was a factory worker in Fujian, a province in South China. She began writing poetry as a hobby, was encouraged when her first poems were published and eventually took a university course in Chinese language and literature. She is now one of China's best known younger poets. As well as patriotic pieces like *My Motherland, Dear Motherland*, which appears here, she has written many love lyrics. Her work shows an accomplished and original use of language and a sophisticated grasp of form and technique.

Shu Ting

My Motherland, Dear Motherland

I was an old dilapidated water-wheel on your banks,
Creaking many weary songs for hundreds of years.
I was the smoke-blackened miner's lamp on your forehead,
Lighting the way when you sprawled in the tunnel of history.
I was the blighted rice ear, the road in need of repair,
The barge run aground on shoals,
with the tow-line deeply, deeply
    Cutting into the flesh of your shoulders,
    —O motherland!

I was poverty,
I was grief.
I was your painful hope
    From generation to generation,
Flowers from the sleeves of flying *Apsaras*
    Which had not touched the earth for thousands of years,
    —O motherland!

I am your new ideal
Just freed from the cobweb of myth.
I am your lotus seed under a quilt of snow,
Your dimples stained with tears.
I am the new white starting line,
The rosy dawn
    Sending out shimmering rays,
    —O motherland!

I am one of your one thousand million,
The sum total of your nine million six hundred thousand
    square kilometres.
With your breasts, covered with wounds,
You fed me,

A girl who was perplexed, pensive and fervent.
Now, derive
From my flesh and blood
Your prosperity, your glory, your freedom,
   —My motherland,
  Dear motherland!

This Is Everything, Too
—Reply to a young friend

Not all giant trees
  Are broken by the storm;
Not all seeds
  Find no soil to strike root;
Not all true feelings
  Vanish in the desert of man's heart;
Not all dreams
  Allow their wings to be clipped.

No, not everything
  Ends as you foretold!

Not all flames
  Burn themselves out
  Without sparking off others;
Not all stars
  Indicate the night
  Without predicting the dawn;
Not all songs
  Brush past the ears
  Without remaining in the heart.

No, not everything
  Ends as you foretold!

Not all appeals
  Receive no response;
Not all losses
  Are beyond retrieval;
Not all abysses
  Mean destruction;
Not all destruction
  Falls on the weak;

Not all souls
   Can be ground underfoot
   And turned into putrid mud;
Not all consequences
   Are streaked with tears and blood
   And do not show a smiling face.

Everything present is pregnant with the future,
Everything future comes from the past.
Have hope, struggle for it,
Bear these on your shoulders.

To the Oak

If I love you—
I'll never be like a campsis flower,
Displaying myself on your high branches;
If I love you—
I'll never mimic the infatuated birds,
Repeating the same monotonous song for green shade;
Or be a spring,
Gushing cool comfort;
A perilous peak,
Enhancing your height and dignity.
Unlike the sunlight,
Unlike spring rain;
None of these suffice!
I must be a kapok tree,
The image of a tree by your side.
Our roots, closely intertwined below,
Our leaves, touching in the clouds.
When a gust of wind brushes past,
We will greet each other,
No one else can
Understand our language.
You'll have bronze branches, an iron trunk,
Like knives, swords and halberds;
I'll have my large red flowers,
Like sighs, heavy and deep,
Or valiant torches.
Together, we'll share
The cold storms and thunderbolts,
Together, we'll share
The mist, rosy clouds and rainbows.
It seems we'll always be separate,
Yet we'll depend on each other.
Only this can be called profound love,
Wherein lies the faithfulness:

Loving not only your greatness,
But also the place where you stand,
The earth beneath your feet!

Translated by Hu Shiguang

Huang Yongyu

Professor Huang Yongyu is not a poet by trade but an artist. He writes occasional verse in much the same way that many Chinese artists, scholars and even statesmen do. He is unusual, in choosing to write in the modern idiom. Others, among them such well known figures as Mao Zedong, Zhou Enlai, Chen Yi and Dong Biwu preferred to use the traditional Song and Tang dynasty forms for their poetry. Professor Huang is one of modern China's five or six finest artists. He is not a Han Chinese but is the best known son of a tiny, ethnic minority people located in the far west of Hunan province, the Tujia. They number a mere four or five hundred households in all. He began his work as a woodblock print artist and still teaches this specialized art form at the Beijing College of Art, where he is a professor. He has greatly broadened the scope of his own art however and now mostly paints using a variety of media, both traditional ink on paper and Western oils and acrylics, to produce innovative works which are a blend of both cultures.

The short poems in his two or three slim volumes of verse are often satires. They are prompted by the memory of his sufferings during the Cultural Revolution, or like the three included here, they display his sharp observations of the less creditable aspects of the bureaucracy at that time. As such they are typical of a brief phase, in 1979–80, when a good deal of such verse appeared.

Huang Yongyu

A Hundred Times Tastier Than MSG
—Three satirical poems

Such a Lovely Smile

Fawning and flattery
Will only create debased happiness.
A humourless remark
From the leading cadre,
Makes him
Double up with
Laughter.
Such a resonant guffaw
Such an animated pose.

He is sure
This will make the cadre happy.
Only he knows how to interpret
The profundity of the boss's words and philosophy.

Better to Hang Him Outright
—Scherzo* in the key of D

While he was alive,
He was busy being envious,
Busy doing people down.
With the result that he achieved nothing;
Has left behind just a few tatty books.

Then,
He felt rich and replete
Because he had within his grasp
Friends' innermost secrets,
That could be sold at any time.

Now
All that has gone out of fashion.
He idles around the streets
Like an unemployed
Othello.

Everyone is working away, laughing, singing,
But he is as poor as a church mouse,
Not knowing how he will eke out
The rest of his days.

Actually
He hasn't really died
This is just a little notion of mine—
Better to hang him outright.

* *Xiéxùque*, the Chinese for scherzo, is a *double-entendre—xiéxuè* means *banter*.

A Hundred Times Tastier than MSG
—*To the leading cadre*

Don't believe what he says.
The fellow smiles so sweetly—
A hundred times tastier than MSG,
If I were you,
I'd boot him out the door.

He hovers around you,
Collecting up for you
    The things you can't get at;
Finding out for you
    The gossip you can't come by.

When you're old, you'll be in his power;
He is your vitamins,
He is your heart pills,
When your brain won't respond to signals,
Your hand and feet begin to fumble,
Don't you worry a bit,
He'll do it all for you;
Just as though, you yourself
                Were out there.

He gives you
A kind of imperceptible spiritual massage.

Until finally,
His brain
                Replaces yours.
His thoughts sit astride your words.
He causes you gradually
                to complete a monumental regression
He has means of making you
                Enjoy
                Numbing grandeur

Until, in the end, politically,
            He has sucked your bones dry of marrow.

Those he hates,
He says are running you down,
If he has no news to offer you
He hardens his heart
            And invents a few stories.

He's turned you
            Into
            Cicada slough discarded in the mud.
Wearing your skin,
He swaggers about swindling one man here, another there.

The day may come,
Possibly,
When you find out this rogue
Is a bit out of line;

Yet you will still feel,
Between you
There exists
An inexplicable entanglement.
By that time
You'll have no way
To counter him;
It's like swallowing a fish-hook,
It gets stuck in one's gut.

Comrade,
Open your window,
Let the fresh air
And sunshine in!

Afterwards,
With one vicious kick
Kick him in the arse.
Kick the toady,
Kick him
Right out the door.
Let him find no new
Ricebowl anywhere!

Dear Comrade,
Brave warrior, you've fought your way
Out of a sea of fire,
Work, think
Richly as a golden autumn.
Make him restore
These precious things
        That once were yours.

Throw away the witch's hat,
        The shackles,
        The honey-pot,
He made you wear.

'Chief cadre this, chief cadre that!'
Those corrosive unguents
Ten times more poisonous than opium,
A hundred times tastier than MSG
You've seen a million enemies
Think—
To be trampled underfoot by this fellow
Can't be worth it!

Beijing, Oct.–Nov. 1979.

Translated by Christine Liao

A SHORT BIBLIOGRAPHY

Ai Qing

Ai Qing Xuanji (Selected poems of Ai Qing). Wenxue Yanjiu She, Hong Kong, 1980.

Bai Honghu and Yang Zhao

Jiaotou Chunyu de Miangui (Distant Cassia Drenched with Rain). Zuozhe Chubanshe, Shanghai, 1978.

Ji Xuepei

Liangge Duizhang (Two Brigade Leaders, Collection of Short Stories), 1961.

Jiang Zilong

'Yige Gongchang Mishu de Riji' (A Factory Secretary's Diary). *Xingang* (New Harbour), No. 5, 1980.

Li Huiwen

'Yizhang Bugao' (A Poster). *Saren Xiaqi* (Chess for Three), 1979.

Liu Fudao

'Nanhu Yue' (The Moon on the South Lake). *Renmin Wenxue* (People's Literature) No. 7, 1980.

Malqinhu

'Huofuo de Gushi' (Story of the Living Buddha). *Peoples Daily*, 12 July 1980.

Shen Rong

'Ren dao Zhongnian' (At Middle Age). *Shouhuo* (Harvest) No. 1, 1980.

Sun Yuchun

'Jiuhou Tu Zhenyan' (In Vino Veritas). *Anhui Wenxue* (Anhui Literature) No. 4, 1979.

Wang Meng

'Shuoke Yingmen' (A Spate of Visitors). *Renmin Wenxue* (People's Literature), 12 January 1980.

Zhang Lin

'Moshengren' (The Stranger). *Beifang Wenxue* (Heilungjiang) No. 1, 1980.

Glossary of Chinese Titles

Stories

Bai Honghu and Yang Zhao   Hansuai, the Living Ghost
柏鸿鹄, 杨昭   勐别姑娘

Ji Xuepei   Two Brigade Leaders
吉学霈 两个队长

Jiang Zilong   Pages from a Factory Secretary's Diary
蒋子龙 一个工厂秘书的日记

Li Huiwen   A Poster
李惠文 一张布告

Liu Fudao   The Moon on the South Lake
刘富道 南湖月

Malqinhu   The Story of a Living Buddha
玛拉沁夫 活佛的故事

Shen Rong   At Middle Age
谌容 人到中年

Sun Yuchun   In Vino Veritas
孙玉春 酒后吐真言

Wang Meng   A Spate of Visitors

王蒙　说客盈门

Zhang Lin   The Stranger

张林　陌生人

Poetry

Ai Qing   The Colosseum of Ancient Rome

艾青　古罗马的大斗技场

Ai Qing   Burnt Out

艾青　烧荒

Ai Qing   Monument to Death

艾青　死的墓碑

Ai Qing   Echo

艾青　回音

Ai Qing   Hope

艾青　希望

Ai Qing   The Mountain Wind

艾青　山风

Ai Qing   Spirits

艾青　酒

Ai Qing   The Wall

艾青 墙

Huang Yongyu   A Hundred Times Tastier than MSG

黄永玉   比味精鲜一百倍

Shu Ting   My Motherland, Dear Motherland

舒婷 祖国啊, 我亲爱的祖国

Shu Ting   This is Everything, Too

舒婷 这也是一切

Shu Ting   To the Oak

舒婷 致橡树